Iceland   W9-BKY-674

Gabriele and Christian Handl

Iceland

49 selected hiking tours on the
island of fire and ice

With 69 color photos,
2 walking maps with a scale of 1:250,000,
1 walking map with a scale of 1:125,000,
24 walking maps with a scale of 1:50,000,
1 walking map with a scale of 1:25,000
as well as 1 general map with a scale of 1:2,000,000.

ROTHER · MUNICH

Cover photo:
The Skógafoss in southern Iceland (see tour 1).

Photo opposite title page (page 2):
Rock formation near Vík in southern Iceland.

All photos taken by the authors.

Cartography:
All hiking maps with exception of page 70 (Nature Conservation
Council, Reykjavik) as well as the general maps
© Iceland Geodetic Survey, Reykjavik.

Translation:
Claudia Ade Team, Stuttgart

The descriptions of all the walks given in this guide are made according
to the best knowledge of the author. The use of this guide is at one's
own risk. As far as is legally permitted, no responsibility will be
accepted for possible accidents, damage or injury of any kind.

1st edition 2000
© Bergverlag Rother GmbH, Munich

ISBN 3-7633-4802-6

Preface

Iceland: the island of fire and ice, a land with an almost magical attraction for every lover of nature during a time in history marked by the destruction thereof. Virgin, wild landscapes, enormous glaciers conflicting with powerful volcanoes, an unusual assortment of plants and animals and only few streets which cut across the land guarantee an unforgettable experience for tourists but can also be demanding. To put it provocatively, Iceland is not an ideal country for hikers!

In many areas, there is no infrastructure. There are only few marked hiking trails, few cabins, few bridges across the raging glacial rivers and scarce possibilities for obtaining provisions. Of course, this can also be seen as a challenge and as a basis for experiencing nature in a genuinely pure form.

The true problems are first exposed with a look at Iceland's geology. Since the volcanic land is still active in many places, a correspondingly thin and unstable topsoil exists with an extremely sensitive vegetation which must struggle with the harsh climate of Iceland. Considerable destruction to the vegetation and a great deal of damage to the sensitive layer of moss and the modest forest land can be caused by only a small number of hikers in the wrong places. We will therefore only attempt to present those tours with existing trails in this walking guide.

It is our goal to present trails to the natural beauties of Iceland which are only open to hikers. We have therefore intentionally abstained from recommending tours which are very long because time is especially valuable in Iceland due to unstable weather conditions. Very often, a simple short walk is all that is needed for an unforgettable experience!

For these reasons, we have concentrated on hiking tours in Iceland's national parks which include the most impressive natural landscapes of the country but which also offer a sufficient infrastructure and can be reached easily using public transportation. These are the basic requirements for the tours included in this guide. Additionally, we will give you short descriptions of all of Iceland's regions so that you can decide for yourself which areas interest you the most.

It is our wish that our readers also experience the fascination of Iceland's lava deserts, glaciers, radiant mosses and massive water falls during their hiking tours and that they are as captivated by the landscape as we are.

Gabriele and Christian Handl

Contents

Tourist Information

Using this guide

This guide is divided into four parts in which an introduction to the respective region is given. A map on which the numbered routes are outlined can be found on pages 14/15 and provides a good general overview.

Before the description of each tour, technical information such as access, length, difficulty and character of the tour can be found. Under the heading »Location«, the nearest settlement with shopping facilities is listed. Excerpts from colored maps taken from the Icelandic Geodesic Institute are included with all routes drawn in, so that the acquisition of further cartographic material is unnecessary. At times, we have not included a description of the point of departure if this is included on a different map. Hiking maps, which can easily be found in the Alps, are not available in Iceland. At the present time, no detailed maps are available for many of the regions. In many areas, only editions of maps drawn in the 1930's are available, but these are difficult to read. It must be taken into consideration that in Iceland, maps cannot be updated quickly enough to show the constant geological changes in the landscape.

A simple climbing point descending from the Thórsmörk.

Fording an ice-cold glacial river is especially demanding.

Grade

In order to better assess difficulties which you may encounter, the suggested tours have been given colored route numbers divided into three levels of difficulty explained as follows:

BLUE

These trails are generally well marked, sufficiently wide and usually not very steep. They can therefore be taken with relatively little danger and when the weather is bad. They can also be taken by children and the elderly under normal conditions and without great danger.

RED

These trails are either sufficiently or partially marked, narrow, exposed for short distances or steep and can quickly lead to problems if the weather is bad (please see the special warnings for each individual tour).

BLACK

These trails are predominately or completely unmarked, contain difficult points such as fords or volcanic fields and/or are greatly exposed. In addition, they are mostly very long and present high demands on your sense of direction. Bad weather can greatly lengthen these tours.

Dangers

We have naturally attempted to put together tours in such a way that unnecessary danger can be avoided. However, in Iceland, personal responsibility and the ability to correctly assess dangers is more important than anywhere else. The time needed for a tour is based upon empirically established figures and the most accurate measurements possible, but depends above all on individual abilities.

Constant sudden changes in the weather occur in Iceland and various extreme weather fronts can quickly follow one another. In higher elevations and in the Highlands, snow can cause difficulties during the entire summer when trying to continue a tour. As a general rule, the Icelandic climate can be compared to middle European standards at an elevation of approximately 2000 m. Heavy rainfall as well as the sun's strong radiation can cause glacial rivers to rise very quickly.

For this reason, one can expect delays if a river (with a water temperature of 3–5° C) has to be forded during a tour. When fording a river (never barefoot!), the girdle on your backpack should be unbuckled as a safety measure so that, in case of a fall, you can free yourself quicker. It is therefore also recommended that you carry a small emergency pack on your body.

A good sense of orientation when using maps is absolutely necessary. Very often, tours follow old trails or sheep paths. In order to cope in areas where there are no trails, you should learn to use a map and compass perfectly. If it is foggy, you should wait, if possible, until the fog clears. Using a GPS (after the right amount of practice!) can also be useful.

Particular caution should be taken in hot volcanic zones. Safeguarding measures are only present in the most famous areas in the form of small paths which are restricted by ropes. In solfataric areas, avoid white spots and the rims of ponds filled with boiling sulphuric acid or mud due to a high risk of collapse! Never go too close to a hot spring and pay close attention to the direction of the wind.

You should not rely blindly on the information given to you by Icelanders, even by cabin caretakers. Their respect for safety is different from what is understood in the Alps. In an emergency (climbing accidents and missing persons), there is an Icelandic rescue group: Slysavarnafélagith Landsbjörg, Stangarhylur 1, IS-110 Reykjavik, Tel. 0587-4040. The telephone number for emergencies is 112.

Equipment

Very good shoes with massive rubber soles (volcanic rock is often as sharp as a knife), warm clothing which can be worn in layers (it doesn't have to be fleece — sweaters from Iceland are also warm and water-repellent) and good protection from rain are a must, as well as rain-repellent covering for your backpack. Be sure to pack everything in your backpack a second time in

Hot springs (pictured here: Hveravellir) offer relaxation after a tour.

waterproof bags. A first aid kit and, for »soloists«, signal rockets are recommended, sufficient provisions, drinking water (depending on the region either in abundance or not at all available) are also needed. A staff is also necessary, it is above all a must for crossing rivers. For fording rivers, it is best to use plastic bathing shoes or rubber boots with cuffs that reach over the knees and have massive rubber soles. Such boots are also ideal for hikes on wet days but are not well suited for tours which last for several days because of the weight. High quality camping equipment with a gas or spirit stove (spirit = Rauthspirit, for camping gas, only the smaller canisters are available, otherwise the Primus System is normal), a good mat to sleep on, a warm sleeping bag and tent which can withstand storms.

Considering the numerous thermal baths (»sundlaug«), don't forget to take bathing necessities!

Lighting conditions and colors make Iceland a photographer's paradise, so take enough film and reserve batteries along.

The best times of the year

June to August, whereas very often the Highland areas are not opened until the middle of July. In July, the days are long and the nights short (Iceland is situated just below the polar circle), in September the days are shorter, there are fewer bus connections and often the weather is bad.

Accommodation possibilities

Those people who want to roam through Iceland should plan a camping vacation in advance because in the most beautiful parts of the country, there are normally no hotels and when one can be found, it is generally very expensive.

There are cabins with no service but equipped with good kitchens which must be shared by all guests, but only few of these have a caretaker present in the summer.

The cabins in Thórsmörk and in Landmannalaugar are also popular weekend destinations for native Icelanders. It is therefore recommended that you consult with the responsible clubs and make a reservation.

Each person is only allowed to bring 3 kilograms of food into Iceland. Importing meat products, butter or milk is not allowed. It is best to take dehydrated foods, soups, mixed nuts to snack on and other such foods. In general, only white bread is available. Milk, cheese products and fish (salmon) are of high quality and are rather inexpensive, other basic foods such as rice or noodles are available at approximately the same price as in Germany. Meat, fruit and vegetables however are expensive, alcohol is only sold in special shops or licensed restaurants and is expensive.

Transportation connections

■ **Bus:** In Iceland, there is a surprisingly well-developed network of privately owned bus companies which offer the possibility of choosing many points

Cabin at Hvitárvatn.

of departure and destinations. The bus companies also offer many guided tours in the summer, for example through the Highlands, to Thórsmörk, to Askja or to Landmannalaugar. For the most part, they are the only possibilities of reaching these destinations if you do not have access to a 4-WD-vehicle. Stopovers are generally possible without additional charge; however, such bus tickets are much more expensive than normal bus connections.

We liked the idea of taking a bicycle which could be folded together into a suitcase (with gears) along in a bus. This option makes it possible to take independent shorter excursions. The ring ticket which is offered for busses is not much cheaper than individual tickets.

The starting points for most of the tours listed in this guide can be reached by bus. However, some parts of Iceland are difficult to reach using public transport, but even with your own vehicle, the question arises as to whether or not driving to remote areas is worthwhile due to long distances with poor-quality roads.

■ **Bicycle:** Those who want to experience Iceland by bicycle with a street bicycle and heavy luggage must be true cycling fanatics. The constantly changing and often stormy weather, the great distances and the varying conditions of the streets speak against using the bicycle as a means of transport. Even on the main Ring Road, in some places stones can be thrown into the air by passing cars and many slopes are very difficult for bicyclers. If, for example, you should want to make a »detour« to Landmannalaugar, you should prepare yourself for stretches where you will have to push your bicycle through sand. Those who cleverly combine busses and hiking and rent a bicycle in Mývatn and Reykjavik, where we can recommend riding a bicycle, (compare Tour 26) will certainly see more of the country and its most beautiful sights.

If you are a fan of mountain biking, the raw slopes of Iceland with fields of lava and rivers to be crossed will certainly be a great challenge for you. Those interested should definitely look into the internet page of the Icelandic Mountainbike Club: www.mmedia.is/~ifhk/touring.htm.

■ **Car:** Taking your own car to Iceland is expensive and takes much time (total of one week there and back), but there are of course destinations (also listed in this hiking guide) which can only be reached by car and are well worth the trip. In order to reach the Highlands, at least an old VW van is necessary, a 4-WD-vehicle would be better since there are always fords to cross. Do not underestimate the risks involved! Fatal accidents occur every year. The price of renting a car is very high compared to international standards and insurance also has to be taken into consideration with recreational vehicles.

Hitchhiking is very difficult due to the low amount of traffic. There is a chance, if you try, to organize rides directly at camping grounds.

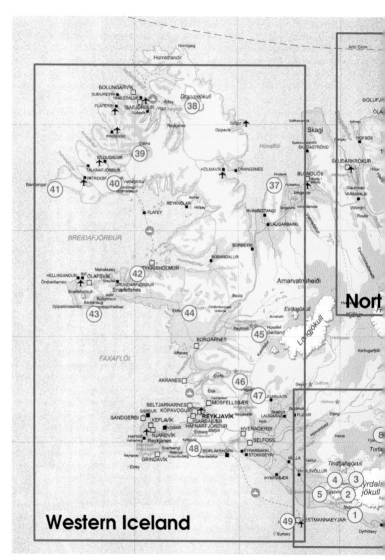

Western Iceland

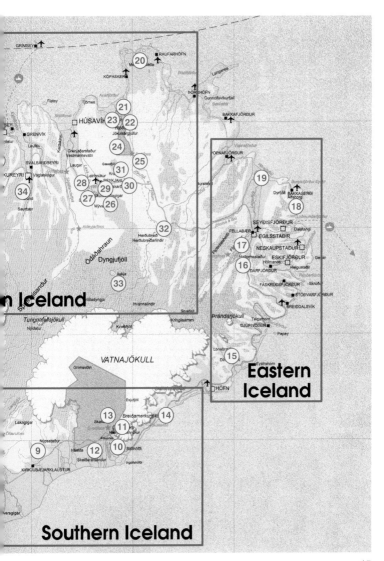

GRIMSEY

RAUFARHÖFN

KÓPASKER

ÞÓRSHÖFN

BAKKAFJÖRÐUR

HÚSAVÍK

GRENIVÍK

SVALBARÐSEYRI

KUREYRI

REYKJAHLÍÐ

Orenjaðarstaður

VOPNAFJÖRÐUR

BAKKAGERÐI
Dyrfjöll Ásbyrgi

SEYÐISFJÖRÐUR

FELLABÆR
EGILSSTAÐIR

NESKAUPSTAÐUR

ESKIFJÖRÐUR

DJÚPIVOGUR

BREIÐDALSVÍK

STÖÐVARFJÖRÐUR

FÁSKRÚÐSFJÖRÐUR

REYÐARFJÖRÐUR

Dyngjufjöll

Askja

Iceland

Tungnafellsjökull

VATNAJÖKULL

Grímsvötn

Eastern
Iceland

HÖFN

KIRKJUBÆJARKLAUSTUR

Skeiðarársandur

Southern Iceland

Walking in Iceland

The land of fire and ice

Iceland is some 300 km east of Greenland in the Atlantic. With 103,000 km² and 265,000 inhabitants, Iceland is an extremely scarcely populated country (2.6 people / km²). The majority of the population lives in cities along the coast, which means that large stretches of land are completely uninhabited. Typical of Iceland are its 140 volcanoes, 30 of which are still active (or possibly are), and their conflict with Iceland's large glaciers. These two elements still shape and change the landscape of this island. One therefore finds vast tundra landscapes as well as high mountains and the largest glaciers in Europe, as well as the largest lava desert on Earth, volcanoes and enormous glacial rivers seeking their way to the sea, unstopped, branching out and only interrupted by waterfalls. The active volcano zone runs from north to south straight through the island, which came into being as a result of the Mid-Atlantic rift. Almost all houses are heated using the natural heat of the Earth and hot springs with no damage to the environment. The positive result is that the air and water in Iceland are left unpolluted.

Tours of several days—long hikes in Iceland

Being exposed to Iceland's overwhelming nature for days or weeks is a fascinating experience but requires high prerequisites both physically and in

Sunrise at Jökulsárlón.

The famous geyser Strokkur is one of Iceland's main tourist attractions.

respect to the necessary equipment. A cross-country camping tour can quickly become a nightmare mainly due to bad weather conditions such as continuous rainfall. Hiking tours along marked trails with the possibility of sleeping in cabins along the way are better. In contrast to the Alps, such trails are more than rare in Iceland and since some cabins are also very small, contact should definitely be made in advance with the hiking club responsible for the cabins. The hiking clubs also offer the following hiking tours (among others) which last for several days, also as guided tours:

■ The trail from Skógar to Thórsmörk and then further on to Landmannalaugar (6 days) is the most beautiful hiking trail known to us. The stages from cabin to cabin (no possibilities for shopping or obtaining provisions!) are: Skógar – Fimmvörthuháls (4 – 5 hrs) – Thórsmörk (compare Tour 1, 5 – 6 hrs) – Emstrur (5 – 6 hrs) – Álftavatn (6 – 7 hrs) – Hrafntinnusker (5 – 6 hrs) – Landmannalaugar (compare Tour 8, 4 – 5 hrs). The trail is marked with posts and some bridges are located along it, but some rivers have to be forded – the hiking times are also dependant on the level of the rivers! Although all of the cabins have space for at least 40 people (since the summer of 1996), it is still necessary to make reservations in advance.

■ From Hveravellir to Hvitarvatn (2 – 3 days, 3 cabins, predominantly a path which can easily be seen) or possibly further to Gullfoss (2 days, no cabins along the Kjalvegur highland area, F 37, no markings).

■ From Snaefell, which lies east of Vatnajökull, over the edge of the Eyjabakkajökull Glacier into the colorful Lónsöræfi Valley on the southern coast (4 cabins, at least 4 days).

- From the cabin at the foot of Herthubreith to Askja (Herthubreitharlindir – Braethrafell i Ódathahrauni – Dreki i Dyngjufjöllum) 2 days, extremely long stages, only partially marked.
- Through the Jökulsárgljúfur National Park, it is possible to hike from Dettifoss via Vesturdalur to Ásbyrgi along the Jökulsá (Tour 22–25). There are camping places but no cabins and the trail is only partially marked.
- In the northernmost part of the Western Fjords, in the 580 km² Hornstrandir Wildlife Preserve, there are several guided tours in the summer, however there are no marked trails. Orientation in this barren landscape is very difficult and boat connections are irregular, even in summer, because of weather conditions. Therefore, it is necessary to plan much time and take food reserves along with you. Hornstrandir has only become an uninhabited area in the last decades after farmers gave up their land. Now the old farmhouses are favorite summer residences for Icelanders. One must be very careful when hiking along the coast because tides can at times make some stretches impassable.
- When taking an extreme tour, you should never underestimate the stretches and should make plans according to accurate maps, take enough food along, inform the police or the caretaker of a cabin before departure and give them your route plans and then of course contact them after returning.

Angelica and field roses grow frequently near water.

Bright green moss covers fossils of leaves (compare Tour 40).

Flora and fauna
Iceland is a nature lover's paradise. The animal kingdom in Iceland is, especially in summer, characterized by numerous brooding birds, seals, reindeer and of course Icelandic ponies which are so popular with by horse riders. There are no poisonous animals on this island, no dangerous animal predators and you can really consider yourself lucky if you should encounter a polar fox. The only animals which are capable of attacking humans are birds which are simply trying to protect their nests (many make their nests on the ground), whereas an (apparent) attack by a scrounger seagull can certainly be frightening. As far as plants are concerned, the crippled growth of many trees such as the birch tree, which rarely reaches a height of over two meters, is very noticeable. Some seem to have evolved into plants which only grow on the ground. Lichen and unbelievably bright moss together with flowers such as the flax with its pink blossoms characterize the flora, often in contrast to the barren volcanic landscape.

National Parks
These are an important element for the preservation of nature on this island because even here, many attempt to exploit the land without taking the environment into consideration. In the national parks, camping is only allowed in allotted areas and hiking should only be done along existing trails. The grandiose nature of the national parks is not their only advantage. Hikers can find well-marked trails here and each park has a national park office which offers weather forecasts, information material, maps and information concerning the conditions of the trails. Usually you can also find a small store or supermarket. If you are travelling by bus, the national parks can be used as a base for several days.

Information and Addresses

Camping
There are about 100 different camping sites with a variety of offerings. With the exception of national parks, setting up a tent in the wilderness is allowed (general rights) but discouraged for environmental reasons. Permission from landowners is required on private property.

Climate
Moderate sea climate with cool summers and mild winters, weather varies greatly, average summer temperature: 10 °C, when the weather is nice, the temperature can rise to over 20 °C but can also go below 0 °C, especially in glacial areas. Weather information in English: Tel. 0902-0600.

Emergencies / Medical attention
Reykjavik: Emergency ward (Slysadeild) at Sjúkrahús Reykjavíkur (City Hospital), Tel. 0525-1000, reachable 24 hrs a day. Telephone number for emergencies: 112.

Festivals
June 17: National Holiday; First Monday in August: bank holiday (favourite day for excursions!).

Getting to Iceland
Regular air connections with Iceland Air, 172 Tottenham Court Road, 3rd floor, London W1P 9LG, Tel. (171) 388-5599, Fax. (171) 387-5711, www.icelandair.com. In the summer, there is a weekly ferry from Esbjerg to Seythisfjörthur (Smyril Line). The journey by ship via Aberdeen – Lerwick – Thorshavn – Seythisfjörthur lasts four days, the return journey takes six days (stay in the Faeroe Islands 2 /3 nights). Information: www.smyril-line.fo and www.poscottishferrries.com.

Hiking clubs
Hiking clubs organize guided hiking tours and have information on capacity and opening hours of the cabins. Since they understandably primarily attempt to sell their own tours and because all cabin caretakers work on a voluntary basis (they are not lessees like in the Alps), the information they give is not always as reliable as you would find in the Alps. Addresses: Ferthafélag Islands, Mörkinni 6 IS-108 Reykjavik, Tel. 0568-2533, www.fi.is; Ùtivist, Hallveigstígur 1, IS-101 Reykjavik, Tel. 0561-4330, www.utivist.is

Information
Ferðamálaráð Íslands, Lækjargata 3, IS-101 Reykjavík, Tel. +354 535 5500,

Fax +354 535 5501, www.icetourist.is.

Language
English is spoken and understood almost everywhere in Iceland, sometimes also German. The Icelandic alphabet has more letters than the German and the following rules for pronunciation apply: There is a voiced and an unvoiced »th« (not differentiated in this hiking guide), ae is pronounced like »I«, á like »(h)ou(se)«, é like »ye«, ó like »o«, u like »ö«, au like »(b)oy«. Some important Icelandic geographical terms are *gil-* gorge, ravine; *gjá* – gap; *hver* – hot spring; *jökull* – glacier; *jökulsá* – glacial river; *vath* – ford.

Leisure activities and Sports
Swimming: There are public swimming pools (sundlaug) in most cities and towns in Iceland which have »hot pots« and whirlpools and can therefore be visited in all kinds of weather. *Riding:* Farms have numerous possibilities and also offer guided tours. Riding equipment must be disinfected after returning. *Fishing:* A permit must be obtained for rivers. Salmon fishing (June – September) must be booked in advance. For trout and char a permit can be obtained at the nearest farm. Equipment must be disinfected. More information can be obtained by contacting The National Angling Association, Bolholt 6, IS-105 Reykjavik, Tel. 354-5531510, fax 354-3684363. *Golf:* Is very popular in Iceland. There are some 28 courses, guests are welcome. *Boating:* Is not allowed even for paddle boats on Mývatn Lake supposedly because of environmental reasons but tours by motor boat are offered. On Jökulsárlón (organized motor boat trips) or on glacial rivers, boating is extremely dangerous and only allowed for »specialists«.

Opening hours of shops
Monday through Friday 9.00–18.00, Saturday 9.00–14.00, some supermarkets daily until 23.00. Many shops are closed on Saturdays during the summer months with the exception of souvenir shops, which are also frequently open on Sundays. Opening hours for banks: Monday to Friday 9.15–16.00, Post Office: Monday – Friday 8.30–16.30.

Telephone
To Iceland from abroad: 00354 (the first number of the city code within Iceland is left off). Important: Telephone books in Iceland are alphabetized according to first names! Code for calling Great Britain: 0044.

Southern Iceland
Thórsmörk – Landmannalaugar – Skaftafell

Colorful rhyolithic slopes mark the landscape around Landmannalaugar.

Easily reached by bus from Reykjavik, southern Iceland offers hikers some of the most beautiful tours and the most impressive landscapes of the island. Only 160 km from Reykjavik, Thórsmörk, which can be compared to an oasis, can be found at the end of the 30 km long Markarfljót Valley. It is better if you come on weekdays because the three cabins with possibilities for camping are a popular weekend excursion place. There is a daily bus connection in the summer. The most impressive and unforgettable way of travelling to Thórsmörk however is by hiking through the Fimmvörthuháls Pass. From Thórsmörk, the enduring hiker can make a four-day tour into the interior of the island to Landmannalaugar (Fjallbak Natural Wildlife Preservation). This preservation, which is north of Mýrdalsjökull, is among the most unforgettable highlights of a trip to Iceland. Even in the days when land was acquisitioned, the »hot springs of the people from the country« were well visited. Hot water with a temperature of up to 72°C mixes with cold water from melting snow and ice in a reservoir which offers a tempting place for long periods of bathing at a temperature which you can choose yourself. In 1979, 47 km^2 were made into a preserve, whereas the exceptional qualities which led to this was not the meagre amount of vegetation with scarcely more than 150 species and the few birds, but rather the colorful rhyolite slopes. On the trails around the camping site, shorter walks and hikes are possible which allow the traveller to obtain a fascinating insight into this region. Good weather and orientation skills are the main prerequisites for tours beyond the markings.

The Skaftafell National Park was founded in 1967 with help from the WWF and currently includes an area of 1600 km². It is an ideal starting point for short and long hikes and offers a camping site, supermarket with restaurant and a national park office as well as a well-developed infrastructure. A lush green crest builds the center of an area which was formed by water and the erosion of glaciers. A bridge was built over the largest glacial river, the Skeithará, in 1974. This national park (open from June 1 to September 15) is located on the Ring Road. There are daily bus connections in the summer from Frykjavik and Höfn.

The edge of the Vatnajökull glacier, blackened by lava ash.

1 Skógar – Fimmvörthuháls – Thórsmörk

Impressive crossing of a pass between waterfalls and glaciers

Skógafoss – Fimmvörthuháls – Morinsheithi – Básar Cabin

Location: Skógar, 20 m, located on the ring road.

Starting point: Skógafoss in Skógar. Approach: There is a bus connection on the Ring Road leaving once daily in both directions.

Walking time: Skógafoss – bridge 3 hrs; bridge – Fimmvörthuháls cabin 1¼ hrs; cabin – Fimmvörthuháls Pass 1 hr; Pass – plateau 1 hr; plateau – Básar cabin 1½ hrs. Total time: 7¾ – 8½ hrs.

Ascent: 1100 m.

Grade: This is a long and strenuous hiking tour. Near the Fimmvörthuháls, the trail crosses a large field of snow which is only marked with a few poles. For this reason, when viewing conditions are not good, severe orientation problems can occur. One point during the descent to Thórsmörk is somewhat distorted.

Accommodation: There is a camping site and a hotel in Skógar. In Thórsmörk, you can find the Básar cabin and camping possibilities.

Alternative route: The tour can be split into a two-day tour by spending the night in the cabin at Fimmvörthuháls. Normally there is no water in the cistern, there are no springs, only snow.

The mighty Skógafoss.

From the Fimmvörthuháls Pass, there is a breathtaking view of Thórsmörk with its bizarre rock formations, its deeply eroded canyons and caverns with waterfalls and the edges of glaciers which reach to the floor of the valley.

To the right of **Skógafoss**, the trail has stairs which ascend upwards and continue along the Skóga River. There are numerous waterfalls over which the water fights its way to the sea. Some smaller secondary valleys can be crossed without problems. You will be so distracted by the beauty of this place that you will hardly notice that you are walking uphill. After 1 hr, you will reach a particularly beautiful waterfall. It is better to take the trail to the right.

The quality of the left trail is not as good and it is steeper, in spite of the fact that it offers a better view. Afterwards, you will cross some streams coming from springs. You should refresh your water supply here. After two more waterfalls, you will reach a crest. After 3 hrs, you will reach a footbridge and cross to the left bank. It is better to follow the street here. The pole markers are intended for the winter. When you see the **cabin**, you can head directly towards it because the street takes a long curve. After a full 4 hrs, you will reach the cabin. This is a good place for a rest. There is a gas jet in the cabin but no stove. From here, the flat ascent to the **Fimmvörthuháls Pass** crosses a field of snow. On the left side, there is a cabin which offers skiing tours in the summer. After 1 hr, we have reached the highest point and begin our descent, although after about ½ hr an easy climbing point which is already equipped with ropes has to be crossed. The trail continues over a plateau mountain, the **Morinsheithi**. After this, you should keep to the left flank of a mountain crest and then hike over a ridge. In places, the trail becomes narrow. On the left is a nice view of Strákagil. Once again you have to make a steep ascent and will arrive at the protected floor of the valley where you will be surprised by lush birch forests. After reaching the river again, a sign points towards the **Básar cabin**, which we can reach in 15 min after crossing a bridge, turning right and then walking along the birch forest.

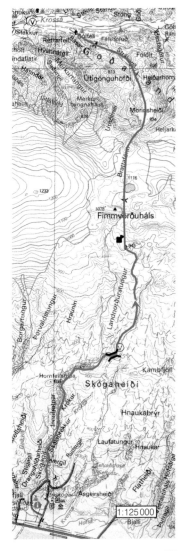

2   The Stakkholtsgjá cavern waterfall

Through Thórsmörk's typical gorge landscape

Básar cabin – Hvannárgil – Hvanná Bridge – Stakkholtsgjá – Básar cabin

Location: Hvollsvöllur, 20 m, located on the Ring Road.
Starting point: Thórsmörk, Básar cabin, 240 m. Approach: Guided tours from Reykjavik, it is possible to join the tour in Hvollsvöllur. Or with a four-wheel drive recreational vehicle (very dangerous street!) on Route 249.
Walking time: Básar cabin – crest ¾ hr; crest – Hvanná bridge ½ hr; Hvanná bridge – entrance to the Stakkholtsgjá gorge ¾ hr;

entrance to the Stakkholtsgjá gorge – cavern waterfall ¼ hr; Stakkholtsgjá cavern waterfall – Básar cabin 1¾ hrs. Total time: 4 – 5 hrs.
Ascent: 150 m.
Grade: Hiking tour on a well-developed and marked trail. Sometimes a shallow ford. Small streams have to be crossed twice on rocks or boards, the last stage to the cavern waterfall is slippery.
Accommodation: Básar cabin or camping.

The destination of this hiking tour is the Stakkholtsgjá Gorge, which is overgrown by the lush green of the mosses and ferns. At the end of this gorge, a waterfall flows from a dim, cavernous area.
To the left of the toilets at the Básar cabin there is a trail which leads through the birch trees. After about 25 min and after we encounter the first crossing point with a signpost, we ascend to the crest in the direction of the **Hvannárgil Gorge**. After about 40 min, we reach the crest (second signpost). From there, the trail goes downhill, whereas you should stay to the right at one point and remain on the trail, which will lead you uphill, and you should not allow yourself to be irritated by some individual pegs along the landscape. At the bottom of the gorge, there is a third signpost. We go through the gorge in

A waterfall pours into the twilight green cavern room of the gorge.

the direction of Álfakirkja. At the end of the gorge, we turn left and cross the **Hvanná River** (bridge). The trail then leads into a road. A stream has to be crossed, depending upon the amount of water either by walking on stones or wading. After 2 hrs, we reach the entrance to the **Stakkholtsgjá Gorge** and cross the stream stepping on stones going to the right side. The gorge makes a heavy turn towards the left and the stream has to be crossed again on boards. On the left, we pass a small cave with beautiful ferns. After ¼ hr, we find a narrow gorge with little water. This gorge has very attractive lighting effects. For the last meters, we climb over smaller cliffs and are then in a cavernous room with its narrow waterfall.

We take the same trail back to the **Hvannárgil**. From there, we first follow the street straight ahead and pass the Alfakirkja rock formations. Shortly afterwards, there is a path on the right which takes us along the bank of the stream and we finally reach the **Básar cabin** again after crossing a footbridge.

3 Gothaland (Tungnakvíslarjökull)

Along raging rivers to the foot of a glacier

Básar cabin – Tungnakvíslarjökull – Básar cabin

Location: Hvollsvöllur, 20 m, located on the Ring Road.
Starting point: Thórsmörk, Básar cabin, 240 m. Approach: Guided tours from Reykjavik, it is possible to join the tour in Hvollsvöllur. Or with a four-wheel drive recreational vehicle (very dangerous street!) on Route 249.
Walking time: Básar cabin – Hruná Bridge 1 hr; Hruná Bridge – saddle ½ hr; saddle –

glacier ¾ hr. Total time: 4½ – 5 hrs.
Ascent: 300 m.
Grade: Marked trail with bridges. Be careful on the edge of the glacier.
Accommodation: Básar cabin and camping.
Alternative route: After the bridge over the Hruná, the trail branches into two further paths to Krossárjökull, approximately 1½ hrs.

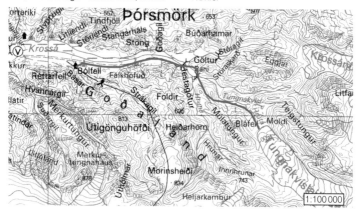

This route will leave you with an impression of how powerful the glacial rivers can be. These rivers originate in Gothaland, the »Land of the Gods« and flow through »Thor's Frontier« (the translation of Thórsmörk).

From the Básar cabin, we travel along the road in the direction of Strakagil and when the road branches off to Fimmvörthuháls, we go straight ahead (east) until we cross the footbridges over the **Hruná** and the **Tungnakvísi**. The footpath leads us to a bright green part of the valley with an elevation of approximately 40 m to a saddle, where we have a splendid view of **Tungnakvíslarjökull**. In this place, a good 1½ hr walk from the cabin, you can experience the mystical feeling of this mighty valley landscape. From here, the trail leads us back down to the stream, which you can hike along to the glacier. The same trail leads back to the cabin.

The glacial river Tungnakvísl runs through the valley.

4 Valahnúkur, 465 m

Short ascent which provides a splendid view

Langidalur cabin – Valahnúkur summit – Langidalur cabin

Location: Hvollsvöllur, 20 m.
Starting point: Langidalur cabin in Thórs-mörk, 220 m. Approach: Guided tours from Reykjavik, it is possible to join the tour in Hvollsvöllur. Or with a four-wheel drive recreational vehicle (very dangerous road!) on Route 249.
Walking time: Cabin – summit 1 hr; summit – cabin ½ hr. Total time: 1½ hrs.
Ascent: 250 m.
Grade: When the weather is good, this is one of the best places for a good view of the valley, the ascent presents no problems.
Accommodation: Cabin in Langidalur, camping.
Alternative route: From the summit hike further north and then turn right and back to the cabin. It takes an extra ½ – ¾ hr.

In spite of what appears to be a very small change in altitude of 250 meters, the Valahnúkur offers one of the most beautiful views in the Thórsmörk. From the summit, you can find a panoramic view of the sea, the Thórsmörk Valley with the many branches of the Krossá River and the glaciers Eyjafjallajökull, Mýrdalsjökull and Tindfjallajökull. This glacial barrier causes a mild climate in the valley but also presents constant danger because there are dormant and unpredictable volcanoes beneath the Eyjafjallajökull and the Mýrdalsjökull.

The **Langidalur cabin**, which belongs to the Icelandic Hiking Club, is at the foot of the Valahnúkur Mountain and is easily reachable on foot from the Básar cabin. You simply have to go along the road past the Álfakirkja and then turn right over the footbridge crossing the Krossá. Do not try taking a short cut! Fording the Krossá can cost you your life!

From the **Langidalur cabin**, you first have to walk across the rather steep meadow of the camping site on the left side of a trench which has birch trees growing in it. You can also go along the right side of the trench, which is somewhat flatter, but then you have to cross to the left side. After the first steep part of the tour, the route is then somewhat flat. The course of the trail is unmarked but can be easily recognized. You should however be careful not to walk too far to the left along the edge of the Krossá. The **summit** is reached in exactly 1 hr.

The **return** is along the same trail.

The many branches of the Krossá characterize the landscape of the Thórsmörk.

5   Glúfrafoss: the hidden waterfall

An interesting detour from the Ring Road

Seljalandsfoss – Glúfrafoss and back

Location: Hvolsvöllur, 20 m.
Starting point: Parking lot in front of the Seljalandsfoss, 40 m. Approach: Bus connections once daily in both directions (Reykjavik – Höfn) on the Ring Road.
Walking time: Seljalandsfoss ¼ hr; to Glúfrafoss and back ¾ hr. Total time: 1 hr.
Ascent: 10 m.
Grade: Wear clothing suitable for rainy weather! Shoes suitable for wading.
Accommodation: In Hvolsvöllur and Skógar.

The waterfalls Seljalandsfoss and Glúfrafoss, which are both located close to the Ring Road, offer a special treat. Whereas it is possible to go behind the 60 m high Seljalandsfoss, the Glúfrafoss is hidden behind a cliff and can only be reached by wading through water.

If you follow the right path from the **parking lot**, you will disappear behind the mighty water curtain of the **Seljalandsfoss** within a few minutes. Gusts of wind can make this excursion into a rather wet occasion and the path is then slippery. Precisely because this is only a short walk from your car, you have to be careful. Good shoes are a necessity for the meadow to the left of the waterfall, but this only puts you in the mood for the Glúfrafoss.

We go back to the road and walk 500 m to the north past a farm. From the street, we can see a narrow, high gap in a cliff. The **Glúfrafoss** is hidden behind this cliff. A path runs over a fence and then leads to the left bank of the stream and through a meadow to this gap in the cliff. The only way to reach the waterfall on foot is to wade through 10 m of a cold but not raging stream and through the gap. At times the water is more than knee-deep. After only a few steps past damp, gloomy walls, a narrow area surrounded by rocks comes into view from which the waterfall flows. It is an impressive picture! (Tips for photos: You will need a tripod. An umbrella is also useful to protect your equipment from mist.) The same path is taken back to the parking lot.

The Glúfrafoss is hidden behind a narrow cliff.

6 Bláhnúkur, 945 m

Along the »burning mountain« to a point with a panoramic view

Landmannalaugar cabin – Bláhnúkur – Landmannalaugar cabin

Location: Hella, Kirkjubaejarklaustur, located on the Ring Road.
Starting point: Camping site or cabins in Landmannalaugar, 600 m. Approach: Landmannalaugar is also reachable by car on the F 22 from the north. Driving the entire stretch along the Eldgja should be reserved for four-wheel drive vehicles. Directly before the camping site, there is a deep ford which requires a suitable vehicle as well as good driving skills to cross. There is also a parking lot before the ford. In the summer, there are daily bus connections from Reykjavik via Landmannalaugar to Skaftafell (this is a guided tour which can be taken in part and during which stopovers are allowed).

Walking time: Cabin – saddle ¾ hr; saddle – ford ¼ hr; river – summit ½ hr; descent ½ hr. Total time: 2 – 2½ hrs.
Ascent: 360 m.
Grade: Crossing a stream, steep, bulky ascent.
Accommodation: In Landmannalaugar: cabins from Iceland's Ferthafélag (115 beds) with cabin caretaker or simple camping site. The »Fjallafang« shop offers provisions and fresh fish from the first of July to the first of September.
Alternative route: Through the Graenagil along the river to the ford, the ascent is about ½ hr shorter.

The active volcanic zone of the **Fjallbak National Park** not only has popular hot springs at the cabins but also offers the many blazing colors of the solfataras at the foot of the »burning mountain«. The diverse colorful impres-

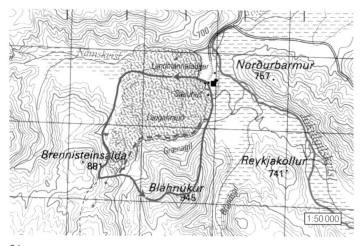

Northern view of Laugahraun from Bláhnúkur.

sions characterize this hiking tour. It begins with the deep black streams of obsidian lava which came into being during the last eruptions in the 16th century and which reach the camping site. At the viewing summit, the red and yellow and even bluish-green colored liparite slopes are striking. Even in summer, they contrast with the fields of snow and present an impressive landscape. Its geological origin is the centrally located Torfajökull Volcano, which caused the largest rhyolithic occurrence in Iceland.

To the right of the cabin at **Landmannalaugar**, a path begins which leads up through this field of lava. This is crossed after about 1 km and the marked trail runs along its edge. It then rises further after 500 m. The **Brennisteinsalda**, the »Burning Mountain«, towers to the right. Caution has to be taken in this area because the active zones and solfataras are not marked or secured. When the trail first branches off to the left, we go straight ahead. After a short, steep ascent directly at the Brennsteinsalda, the path turns left down to the stream, which has to be forded. On the other side, a good view of the **Bláhnúkur** arises. The path is steep and bulky and is therefore difficult to hike. The view becomes more impressive with each meter of higher altitude. At the summit, an orientation disc assists you in making sense of the confusion of the surrounding mountains.

From the summit, the trail descends in a curve along a ridge towards the cabin. The stream, which is some 300 m from the cabin, can be crossed taking a small bridge without getting your feet wet. If desired, you can take the path along the river in order to find a view of the bright green layers of rock of the **Graenagil** at the foot of the Bláhnúkur.

7 Litla Brandsgil – Skalli, 1027 m

Hiking without a trail to a mountain with a magnificent view

Landmannalaugar Cabin – Litla Brandsgil Valley – Skalli – Brennisteinsalda – Landmannalaugar Cabin

Location: Hella, Kirkjubaejarklaustur, located on the Ring Road.

Starting point: Camping site or cabin in Landmannalaugar, 600 m. Approach: Landmannalaugar can be reached by car from the north on the F22. Passage of the entire distance along the Eldgja is reserved for four-wheel drive vehicles. Just before the camping site there is a deep ford, the crossing of which requires a suitable vehicle and correct driving skills. There is however a parking lot before the ford. In the summer, there is a daily bus connection from Reykjavik via Landmannalaugar to Skaftafell (this is a guided tour which can be taken in part and which allows for stopovers).

Crossing a river in the Stóra Brandsgil.

Walking time: Landmannalaugar – branching off of the trail to Stóra Brandsgil/Litla Brandsgil ¾ hr; branch Stóra Brandsgil/Litla Brandsgil – Litla Brandsgil 1¼ hrs; Litla Brandsgil – Skalli 1 hr; Skalli – long trail 1½ hrs; along the long trail to the cabin 1½ hrs. Total time: 6 – 7 hrs.

Ascent: 450 m.

Grade: Since this tour is partially unmarked and leads you along mountain tops and since the path cannot be easily recognized in most places, orientation is only possible under the right weather conditions. In Stóra and the Litla Brandsgil Valley, the river (which is normally shallow and has many branches) must be crossed several times, therefore you should never take this tour when the river is flooded or there is a possibility of flooding. In the higher parts of the valley, fields of snow make hiking easier because you don't have to wade through the river.

Accommodation: In the Landmannalaugar cabin, which belongs to the Icelandic Ferthafélag, and on simple camping sites (shopping possibilities available in summer).

Alternative route: Running parallel to the Litla Brandsgil Valley on the left, a path takes you along a ridge. The river only has to be crossed once. The path returns to the »main trail« below the Skalli Mountain.

This demanding circular hike from the Litla Brandsgil Valley to the viewing point on the Skalli Mountain offers an especially precise insight into the Fjallbak National Park. In the valley, there are no marked paths and several times the river has to be crossed, which is also possible in summer with high rubber boots. You will quickly be convinced that this area lies more than

500 m above sea level which means that the average yearly temperature is only 0°C and snowfall is common in summer. Fascinating rock formations and the unbelievable variety of colors on the walls of the gorge make up for the troubles and raw conditions. The view from the Skalli Mountain, which is 1027 m high, can often reach to Vatnajökull and offers an unforgettable 360° panorama.

We pass the cabin on the left via a footbridge (which also leads to Bláhnúkur) and keep to the left in order to reach the **Stóra Brandsgil**. After about 45 min, the Stóra Brandsgil Valley branches off to the right and can only be followed for several hundred meters. We stay to the left in the **Litla Brandsgil Valley**. Fields of snow usually make hiking here easier. You should, however, only stay on the edges of these fields in order to not break through them. We pass a small waterfall and a gravel shoulder. After 2 hrs, the valley turns to the right. You can see a ridge on the left with a field of snow. Here we climb to the south. The summit of the **Skalli** rises in front of us and we should head for it and will reach it in 1 hr. From the summit, we go in a southwestern direction for about 1 km, then along the ridge to the northwest (do not go to the left or right: deep trenches!). After 1 hr, we reach a noticeable hill on the right side and pass it on the left (there are snow cornices on the right side). You should then see and head for a marking post on another hill. From here, go in a northeastern direction on the well-marked hiking trail **Skógar – Landmannalaugar**, passing the **Brennisteinsalda**, back to the cabin, where the warm pool is a perfect place to relax.

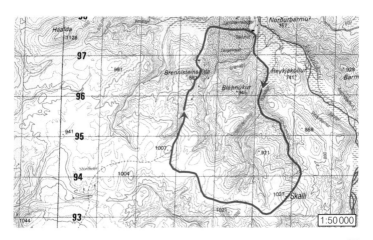

8 Thermal zone at the Hrafntinnusker

Demanding tour to one of the most fascinating thermal areas in Iceland

Landmannalaugar – Brennisteinsalda – Hrafntinnusker – Landmannalaugar

Starting point: Cabin or camping site in Landmannalaugar. How to get there and town/village see Tour 7.
Walking time: Ascent 4 hrs; thermal zone 2 – 4 hrs; descent 3 hrs. Total time: 9 – 11 hrs.
Ascent: 600 m.
Grade: Basically a long hiking tour. The rounds of the thermal zone are not marked and have no paths. Do not go too close to solfataras, steaming hot springs or mud holes as there is a danger of them collapsing! Fields of snow!
Accommodation: Cabins and camping sites in Landmannalaugar, two cabins with a total of 40 beds at Hrafntinnusker.

This long and demanding hiking tour leads us to a mountain made of obsidian and to an area behind the mountain with numerous hot springs, solfatatas, mud holes, ice caves and even a geyser. The most noticeable thing about this area is a 50 to 100 m high column of steam which can be seen and heard from a great distance. Good weather is essential for this tour, as there are no trails.

The thermal zone – the column of steam can be clearly recognized.

As with Tour 6, we begin at **Landmannalaugar**. However, at **Brennistein-salda**, you do not go left, but instead straight ahead climbing higher and higher on the trail, which is marked with posts. After 7 km, we pass some solfataras. After another 2 km, the trail crosses a field of snow on a flat saddle.

When foggy, two people are often necessary for orientation because of the often chaotically spread out signs and the great distance between stakes. One person must look for the next marker and remain in vocal contact with the other. After this field of snow, the Hrafntinnusker, which is completely made of obsidian, can be seen on the right. After exactly 1 km, two small cabins can be found. Here we leave the marked trail and cross this black obsidian hill going west. From this point, there are no more paths.

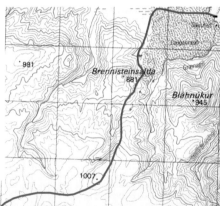

The solfataras, mud holes and ice caves, which are worth seeing, can be found in a valley which runs from north to south behind the Hrafntinnusker.

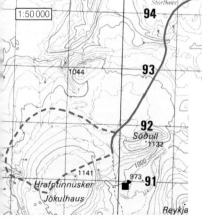

The column of steam is in the southern part of the valley.

For your return, it would be best to follow the valley and circle in a northeasterly direction until you find the marked trail again. You can then hike back to Landmannalaugar with no problems.

9 Kirkjubaejarklaustur

A pleasant circular route to the »Basalt Church Cobblestones«

Kirkjubaejarklaustur – Systravatn – »Church Cobblestones« and back

Location: Kirkjubaejarklaustur, 50 m.
Starting point: The west end of Kirkjubaejar-klaustur. To the right of the slaughter house (parking possibility) there is a gate. The trail begins here. Approach: Bus connection once daily in both directions (Reykjavik – Höfn) on the Ring Road.
Walking time: 1¼ – 1½ hrs.
Ascent: 140 m.
Grade: A steep ascent at the beginning, otherwise a pleasant hike with good views.
Accommodation: Edda Hotel, camping site, hotels in Kirkjubaejarklaustur.

The name of the town of Kirkjubaejarklaustur, which is very difficult to pronounce, is a reminder of its founding by Irish monks and of a monastery which once existed here. The main attraction of this place has, in spite of its name, a natural origin. The »Church Cobblestones« consist of orderly formed columns of basalt.

Going through the gate, the well-built trail, which is marked with red stakes, initially rises steeply through a forest and passes a waterfall on the left. After an ascent of 130 m, you reach a patch of grass with the **Systravatn** Lake. On a clear day, you can see as far as Vatnajökull and across the Nýja-Eldhraun. The path then leads in a northeasterly direction for some 1.5 km along a steep break. The descent begins at a wall of basalt with beautiful formations. It follows a good path downhill in stages until you reach a private house on the left at the bottom. Over a crossing, you will pass a road which you then follow to the right. After a short amount of time, you reach a parking lot. From

The »Church Cobblestones«.

here, a path branches off through a gate and leads to the famous »Church Cobblestones«. From here, you either go back to the road or continue over the meadow towards a wooden fence, which you will have to climb over. You will then find yourself on the local road which leads you back to the starting point.

The trail leads up from the waterfall.

10 Skaftafell National Park

Pretty walking tour to the Svartifoss, which is surrounded by basalt columns

Skaftafell National Park – Svartifoss – Hundafoss – Thjófafoss – Skaftafell National Park

Location: Skaftafell National Park and camping site, 100 m, open from June 1 to September 15, bus stop on the Reykjavik – Höfn line.
Starting point: Camping site. The trail begins at the western end of the site.

Approach: Route 1; bus connection.
Walking time: 1½ hrs.
Ascent: 150 m.
Grade: A nice walk.
Accommodation: Camping site in the Skaftafell National Park.

From the camping site, the wide trail rises to **Svartifoss**, which is one of the most popular photographic motives in the national park due to the basalt columns which overhang and frame the waterfall. These columns are formed if a stream of lava cools down and declining crevices occur. The top layer mainly consists of irregularly formed columns (»fake lava organ«), the lower layers are almost perfect columns, the so-called true lava organ. This is one of the few places in Iceland which is overwhelmed by tourists, but the tour groups usually disappear as quick as they come. Therefore, if you are a little patient, this natural jewel can be enjoyed in peace.

From here, we cross the stream and walk towards **Sjónarsker**. Shortly before reaching Sjónarsker, we turn left at the crossing and soon come back

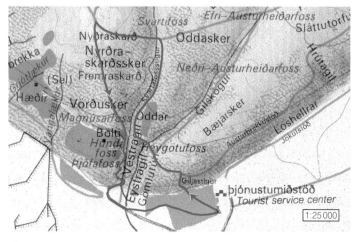

to Stórilaekur Creek, which we then follow. The **Hundafoss** and the **Thjófafoss** are two more beautiful waterfalls along this trail. We come back to our starting point by crossing a street bridge.

The Svartifoss falls over hanging basalt columns.

11 Skaftafellsjökull

An easy walk to the foot of the mighty glacier

Skaftafell – Skaftafellsjökull – Skaftafell

Location: Skaftafell National Park and camping site, 100 m, open from June 1 to September 15, bus stop along the Reykjavik – Höfn line.
Starting point: Tourist Service Center. Approach: Route 1; bus connection.
Walking time: 1 – 1½ hrs.
Ascent: None.
Grade: A beautiful walk also possible in bad weather.
Accommodation: Camping site in the Skaftafell National Park.
Alternative route: Climbing the glacier is possible on guided tours. Those who want to try it on their own definitely need a pick, crampon, and the necessary experience. The border of the glacier is deeply fissured after several hundred meters.

The edge of the glacier in Skaftafell as well as Morsárjökull and Skeitharárjö-kull (which is the largest valley glacier in Europe) characterize the landscape of this national park with their rivers, which have in turn created immense piles of sand. The trail is well travelled and along its way you can also clearly see a great variation of vegetation. The varying conditions in this area, which include gravel surfaces, moorlands and birch forests, make it a home to a wide variety of bird species, above all the yellowhammer, the common snipe, the meadow pipit and the wren. The Skeitharársandur is an important nesting area for scavenger seagulls. This hike is especially suitable for cloudy days.

The well-used path begins after a road east of the restaurant. It leads through a birch forest, but mainly over the massive sand piles of the **Skaftafell Glacier**, which is partially colored black by the volcanic ash. The glacier is not steep, but climbing is only possible with the correct equipment because a steep stony ridge has to be climbed.

From the glacier, you can either turn and go further south or take the trail back.

Volcanic ash has colored the Skaftafellsjökull black.

12 Morsárdalur

Through the birch forests of the Skaftafell National Park

Skaftafell National Park – Hundafoss – Sjónarsker – Monsárdalur

Location: Skaftafell National Park and camping site, 100 m, open June 1 to September 15. Bus stop on the route Reykjavik – Höfn.
Starting point: Camping site, the trail begins at the western end of the site. Approach: On Route 1; bus connection.
Walking time: Camping site – Sjónarsker ½ hr; Sjónarsker – Morsárdalur 1 hr; Morsárdalur – camping site 1¾ hrs. Total time: 3 – 3½ hrs.
Ascent: 200 m.
Grade: Take along a staff and secure shoes.
Accommodation: Camping site in Skaftafell National Park.
Alternative route: From Hundafoss to Svartifoss, over the footbridge to the viewpoint Sjónarsker, additional ¼ hr.

The trail leads through a moorland at the beginning and then down through a birch forest where the trees grow higher and higher due to the milder climate. This climate was the reason for early settlement of the area. Skaftafell is a place where the Icelandic parliament and court used to convene. Mainly due to the fact that grazing by sheep was stopped with the formation of the national park, birch trees and mountain ash trees which reach a height of 2 m as well as bellflowers, wilted sax, forest cranesbill and true angelica also grow here. A variety of insects are also noticeable here, you can even find butterflies.

Leaving the camping site, we walk along the marked, wide trail along the **Hundafoss** to the **Sjónarsker** viewing point. From there, we take the trail going to **Morsárdalur** (Göngubru á Morsá-Kjos). After 1¾ hrs, we reach a bridge over the Morsá. This river comes from the Morsárdalur with its hanging glaciers and the Kjos, where colorful rhyolith mountains and hot springs can be found. Before the bridge, a path branches off to the left which leads along the river. In 1994, there was a sign stating that the path was dangerous. The trail leads us mostly through thick birch forests and is narrow, but it is well trampled down and has some sloping, exposed spots. Again and again, there are beautiful views of the Morsá River. We go past smaller, idyllic waterfalls until we finally, after 1½ to 1¾ hrs, reach a typical national park trail (steps, stakes). The administrators of the national park appear to be in the process of reconstructing the trail, making it (overly) wide. If we go towards the east, past a shed and along a street across a bridge, we return to the camping site.

On the return path, we pass idyllic waterfalls.

13 Kristínartindar, 1126 m

To the summit between the glaciers

Skaftafell National Park – Sjónarnípa – Gláma – Kristínartindar – Nyrthrihnukur – Sjónarsker – Skaftafell National Park

Location: Skaftafell National Park and camping site, 100 m, open from June 1 to September 15, bus stop on the Reykjavik – Höfn line.
Starting point: Camping site, the trail begins at the Western end of the site. Approach: On Route 1; bus connection.
Walking time: Camping site – Sjónarnípa viewing point 1 hr; Sjónarnípa viewing point – Glárna viewing point 1½ hrs; Glárna viewing point – Kristínartindar 1½ hrs; Kristínartindar – Nyrthrihnukur ½ hr; Nyrthrihnukur –

On the way to Kristínartindar.

Sjónarsker 1½ hrs; Sjónarsker – camping site ½ hr. Total time: 7 – 8 hrs.
Ascent: 1050 m.
Grade: Long hike, steep ascent through cliffs and gravel, can only be recommended during good weather, whereas even then, strong winds can prevent climbing.
Accommodation: Camping site in the Skaftafell National Park.
Alternative route: Directly behind the Tourist Service Center, a path (Austurbrekkuslòth) leads along a slope leading to the Sjónarnípa viewing point, 1 hr walking time.

The summit of the Kristínartindar rises high between the edges of the Vatnajökull Glacier and offers a breathtaking view of the surrounding mountains and enormous piles of sand. From the Sjónarnípa viewing point we have an unimaginably beautiful view of Iceland's highest mountain, the Hvannadalshnúkur, which towers majestically over the Skaftafellsjökull.

10 min from the **camping site**, we reach the branch to the right leading to the Sjónarnípa viewing point. The trail first takes us through a birch forest and then crosses an open moorland. On our left, a stream with smaller waterfalls accompanies us on our way. After 1 hr, we reach a signpost showing us the way to the **Sjónarnípa** viewing point. From here, we walk uphill further north and in almost exactly 1 hr we reach the **Gláma** viewing point (650 m). Up to this point, we have already climbed 550 m. A mountain with two projecting peaks rises to the north. An easily recognized path branches off from the

After the summit (in the foreground), the ridge cannot be crossed.

View of Hvannadalshnúkur, the highest mountain in Iceland.

main trail to the right. The trail ascends steeply through rocky terrain and leads us to the first of the **Kristínartindar Summits** (979 m) after ¾ hr.

Afterwards, the trail descends 50 m into a saddle before the path again takes a zigzag ascent and then splits. (The left path along the ridge appears to be the best.) It's a rocky path and we sometimes find that we go »two steps forward, one step back«, but there are no difficult climbs which have to be made. When we finally reach the top, we have a magnificent view of the surrounding mountains, the edges of the glaciers and sand piles. In overview, we recognize here the power of the glacial streams (Jökulhaups) of the **Skeithará River**. They appear approximately every 5 years, causing the river to swell from 200 m³ to 7400 m³ per second. The reason for this are the volcanoes, which still change the appearance of the national park.

The **descent** follows the same path back to the saddle. We stay to the right and follow the path through the corrie down to the main trail. Here, you can quench your thirst at a small stream and the meadow is an inviting place for a nap. A very short ascent brings us to the **Nyrthrihnukur** viewing point. From here, the path passes picturesque ponds with cotton grass, down to the **Sjónarsker** viewing point and further back to the camping site.

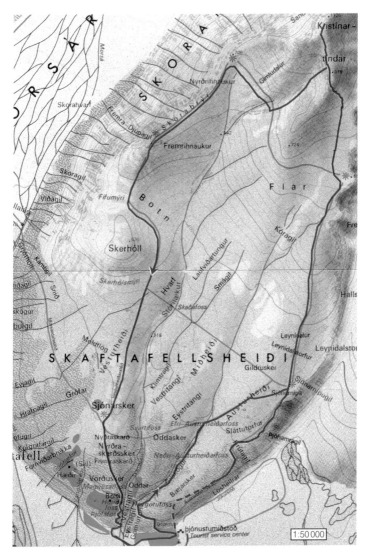

14 Jökulsárlón

A hike along the shore of Iceland's most famous glacial lake

Bridge – lake and back

Location: Skaftafell or Höfn.
Starting point: Parking lot on both sides of
the Ring Road. Approach: Bus connection
on the Ring Road once daily in both
directions.
Walking time: Southwestern shore approximately 4 km, there and back 3 – 3½ hrs;
Eastern shore 3.5 km, there and back 2½ –
3 hrs.
Ascent: 20 – 30 m.
Grade: Be careful about attacking seagulls,
especially on the eastern shore of the lake.
Holding a staff over your head is helpful in
case of an (apparent) attack by a seagull.
Accommodation: On the western shore of
the lake, you can set up a tent. Caution: no
drinking water!
Advice: Sunrise over the Jökulsárlón Lake is
one of the most beautiful experiences in
Iceland.

Many tourists only stop at Jökulsárlón for a half hour to take pictures or take
an organized boating tour on the lake, whereas the noise of the boats is
rather unpleasant. It is much more pleasant to spend the night here (weather
permitting) in order to enjoy the entire tranquillity and beauty of the lake. The
icebergs have a variety of colors from white to blue to black, the latter being
colored by the ashes of nearby volcanoes. The positioning of the icebergs
constantly changes.

You can walk along both shores of the lake with no problems because on
both sides of the outlet and near the bridge, well used but unmarked paths
begin. You can also find parallel paths. Out of respect for the vegetation, you
should always stay on the paths. If you go along the eastern shore past the
boathouse, you can reach the edge of the glacier, which runs flatly into the
moraine. We discourage climbing the glacier without suitable equipment.

The breeding grounds of the large scavenger seagull is at the edge of the
glacier. They nest from May to June. You should always avoid this area
because the birds are known to attack.

The Jökulsárlón Lake with a view towards Vatnajökull.

Eastern and Northern Iceland
Fjord landscape around Egilstathir

An impressive fjord landscape in the east and southeast of Iceland welcomes travellers who arrive in Seythisfjörthur by boat. The Eastern Fjords are considered to be the oldest part of Iceland. Their sharp ridges rise ruggedly from the sea with a height of 1300 m, the »Icelandic Alps«. Positioned along this coast, there are several smaller islands such as Skrúthur and Papey, which are populated by birds. In the south, there is an even coast with a lagoon ceding from the sea which offers ideal conditions for eider ducks, grey geese and singing swans. Although the Ring Road is not paved in the area of the Eastern Fjords and runs past the steep cliffs and a strong rainfall can easily make the road unpassable, this area is particularly interesting, especially for geologists. Here you can find zeolite as well as jasper and agate, for example at the Teigarhorn farm, which of course is strictly protected.

The rocky towers of the Hérathsflói Bay (Tour 19).

A walk along the beach at Hérathsflói Bay.

An ideal starting point for discovering eastern Iceland is Egilsstathir, which was founded in 1945 and lies within a large agricultural area and has a good infrastructure. Going southwest from Egilsstathir, you can take a tour around Lagarfljót, a channel lake from the ice age. Behind the lake, Snaefell (1833 m), the highest mountain in eastern Iceland, rises and can easily be reached with only a four-wheel drive vehicle. Herds of reindeer graze at its foot. There is also a mountain cabin here in which 62 people can sleep and from which guided hiking tours can be taken into the spacious (320 km²) Lónsöraefi Nature Preserve. This area spans from Snaefell to Vatnakökull and the southern coast and is known for its colorful liparite mountains. North of Egilsstathir, there are widely stretched bays such as Hérathflói, where numerous waders and grey geese can be found. The interior parts of the island along the Ring Road towards the west are characterized by a lonely, monotone tundra. Only after seeing the now uninhabited Jökulsdalsheithi can you really understand Halldor Laxness' novel »His Own Lord«.

Hiking possibilities in this fully enchanting area are spread across large areas which means that you will usually need your own vehicle in order to reach the starting points.

15 Liparite mountains at the Hvannagil gorge

A difficult cross-country tour through colorful mountains of debris

Holiday settlement – Seldalur – Hvannagil – holiday settlement

Location: Stafafell, Höfn.
Starting point: From Stafafell, a slope runs along the right side of Jökulsá past several holiday homes. After 3 km, there is a parking lot in front of a small bridge. Approach: On the Ring Road; bus connection from Höfn and Egilsstathir to Stafafell.
Walking time: Bridge – basalt wall ½ hr; basalt wall – ridge ¾ hr; ridge – viewing point at Hvannagil 1¼ hrs; Viewing point – Jökulsá ¾ hr; Jökulsá – bridge 1 hr. Total time: 4¼ – 4¾ hrs.
Ascent: 120 m.
Grade: Unmarked trail, crossing of streams, difficult orientation during bad weather conditions.

Accommodation: Camping and accommodation in Stafafell.

1:100 000

This lonely landscape in the catchment area of Jökulsá i Lóni is particularly fascinating for those hikers who are interested in geology. Liparite, resp. rhyolite, is lava with a high percentage of silicic acid, which results in a bright color. Here you can find yellow (sulphur), red (iron) or white (gypsum) scoria on piles of debris.

At the bridge, we climb uphill along the right side of the **Seldalur Valley** stream. A curve in the stream is crossed along a black water pipe because the stream flows close to the cliffs. We then go further on the left side of the stream through birch undergrowth. After ½ hr, the valley becomes rockier and narrower. It passes a double basalt wall. Behind a bend to the right, a striking rock formation appears. Afterwards, we again cross the stream to the right bank and walk along a slope of rubble. As soon as you can see a waterfall, the stream is crossed again. You then climb the slope on the left side. After a total of 1¼ hrs, you come to a sort of high plateau which you follow in a northwestern direction along the stream. Here you are aided by sheep paths. Ahead there is an impressive panorama of colorful liparite mountains.

Arriving at the watershed, you can make your way across the fields of debris (however only if viewing conditions are good) to a striking rock formation in **Hvannagil** in order to reach a good viewing point. We then hike along the ridge of the Hvannagil Valley to Jökulsá. We go behind a summit with striking red rocks and can then descend to the bottom of the Hvannagil Valley over a shoulder and field of debris before the gorge leads into Jökulsá after a narrow pass. When the water level is normal, you come to the left bank, past rugged cliffs, to the **Jökulsá** field of debris and then encounter a slope which you can follow back to the **starting point**, 4 km to the southeast.

View of Hvannagil and Seldalur in the direction of Lónsöraefi.

16 Forest at Hallormsstathur

A short walk through one of the rare Icelandic forests

Parking lot – educational path – parking lot

Location: Egilsstathir, 80 m.
Starting point: 1 km after the Edda Hotel Hallormsstathur (Route 931) there is a small parking lot on the left, to the right the sign »Trjasafn – Gönguleith«. Approach: Bus connection only Wednesdays from Egisstathir, 18.30 back from Edda Hotel.
Walking time: ½ – ¾ hr.
Ascent: 40 m.
Grade: Walk, wide, marked trail.
Accommodation: Hallormsstathur, camping, Edda Hotel.
Alternative route: After the camping site, there is a branch going towards Atlavik, to the right, the sign »Guttormslundur« points towards the tallest tree in Iceland, 10 min further.

Before settlement, 20 % of Iceland was covered with low-growing forests, but due to clearing and especially due to overgrazing, this area was reduced to 2 % in the past century. First attempts to protect the forests began in 1899, among others here in Hallormsstathur. The area which is now forest land includes almost 2000 hectare, of which the 2-hectare large planting garden is an important element. Five and a half million plants have come from here in the past 80 years.

In front of the **parking lot**, you go through a **gate** on the right side of the street. The trail loops through a forest with surprisingly tall and varied species of trees. Fifty different types of trees grow here. These include 38 conifers like the Sitka spruce, mountainous hemlock spruce and Murray spruce as well as twelve deciduous trees, including the birch, which is the only tree species in Iceland of which there are complete forests, as well as poplars and gray alder brought here from Norway. A favourable condition for this forest is the basalt subsoil with layers of liparite and the loess soil, which when plowed and drained provides an especially fertile soil for Icelandic standards. The information showing the age of the trees is especially interesting and shows that they grow extremely slowly. Along this trail, you also come across a beautiful **picnic meadow**, a popular excursion place for Icelanders.

A comparison shows the sizes of the trees in Hallormsstathur.

17 Hengifoss

Ascent along waterfalls between rhyolith columns

Parking lot – Litlanesfoll – Hengifoss

Location: Egilsstathir, 80 m.
Starting point: Some 30 km from Egilsstathir on Route 931 there is a parking lot on the
northwest shore of the Lögurinn Lake with
toilet facilities and an orientation table.
Approach: Bus connection only on Wednes-
day, back at Edda Hotel in Hallormsstathur
at 18.30.
Walking time: 1½ – 2 hrs.
Ascent: 270 m.
Grade: A small stream has to be crossed.
Accommodation: Egilsstathir, Hallormsstathur.
Alternative route: Climbing on the right
bank of the river.

1:100 000

Hengifoss is considered to be one of the most impressive beauties of nature
in the Egilsstathir region. The 118 m high waterfall is the third largest in
Iceland. From the convenient **parking lot** location, you cross the street, climb
up steps and follow the clearly seen path along the left bank of the river. At
one point, a shallow stream has to be crossed. It is also easy to observe the
vegetation of the drooping meadow with bellflowers, snow gentians, thyme,
moonwort and stemmless toadflax.

After about half of the ascent, you have a good view of the gorge and can see
the Litlanesfoss, which is surrounded by greyish-brown and black basalt
columns. The polygonal columnous forms which are exposed by the water
were caused by contractions and the formation of tears during the cooling
phases of lava. After ascending for a full hour, you will find yourself in front of
the **Hengifoss**, which cascades from the edge of the plateau into the basin
through the walls of the cliffs, which are covered with a bright red layer of
sediment.

The **descent** is made back along the same trail, whereas you have a good
view of the long Lögurinn Lake. This 30 km long lake is 112 m deep (i.e. the
bottom is 92 m below sea level). Its basin shape is a result of the last Ice Age
when it was furrowed by glaciers and then filled by the Jökulsá á Fljótsdal. By
the way, a sea monster (»Lagarfljótsormurinn«) is supposed to live in this
lake.

The Litlanesfoss is encircled by mighty rhyolith columns.

18 Hvituhnjúkur

A lonely hike through rhyolith mountains on the eastern coast

Tangur Valley – Hvituhnjúkur and back

Location: Egilsstathir, Bakkagerthi.
Starting point: Enter the Tungur Valley on Route 946 7 km from Bakkagerthi until a bad slope curves to the left. The 2.5 km to the holiday house can be reached with a car. Approach: Only by car on Route 946.
Walking time: Holiday house – branch in the road ¼ hr; Branch – mountain slope ½ hr; foot – foothill of Hvituhnjúkur 1 hr; along saddle ¼ hr; descent 1 hr. Total time: 3 hrs.
Ascent: 440 m.
Grade: Unmarked, at times no trail, sometimes swampy, stony descent.

Accommodation: In Egilsstathir.

1:100 000

We have intentionally included tours in the Egilsstathir region which can only be reached by car because this region is considered the springboard to the ferry harbors of Seythisfjörthur. The drive to Hérathsflói and further across the pass to Bakkagerthi is worthwhile because of the landscape. Approximately 7 km past the village, the street becomes more than rough. Until the starting point of the tour, it can barely be driven by car. The main attraction of this tour is the stone theater at Hvituhnjúkur, from which you can find a spectacular view of the high, rugged and partially colorful mountains.

From the **starting point**, you follow the road for 15 min and then branch off to the left in order to continue towards the east through a meadow which is partially soaked by ponds. After approximately ½ hr, you turn to the colorful slope on the left and look for a suitable place to climb. After at least 1 hr, you find yourself at the **Hvituhnjúkur** stone theater. We will then return in a western direction and go along the crest until a lake, surrounded by an embankment, appears below on the left. From here, we descend over a stony slope. From the lake, a path leads to the southwest to a fenced-in holiday house. We remain to the left of the fence and climb down the last hill, cross the stream over a bridge thus return back to our **starting point**..

The rugged crest of Hvituhnjúkur as seen across a colorful field or rubble.

19 Hérathsflói bay

A walk along the beach to a colony of seagulls on a colorful cliff

No trail: Choice of a route depends on the tides

Location: Egilsstathir, 80 m.
Starting point: At a curve in the road before Route 917 rises to Hellisheithi after Vopnfjörthur. Approach: Bus connection Mondays and Wednesdays via Vopnaf-jörthur.
Walking time: 1½ – 2 hrs.
Ascent: 30 – 50 m.
Grade: Not marked, only sheep paths, several smaller streams have to be crossed, rubber boots are recommended.
Advice: Take along binoculars, a tripod and a telephoto lens!

The Hérathsflói Bay, where the Jökulsá á Brú and Lagarfljót rivers flow from a 15 km wide valley through a vast alluvial land to the sea, is a particularly interesting destination for ornithologists. While you can observe freeloading scrounger seagulls, singing swans, teals and polar ducks, our tour leads us to a colony of three-toed seagulls at the attractive edge of the bay.

From the **road**, you first go to the northeast along a **lane**, cross a wide but shallow stream and hike across swampy land to the **beach**. Follow the beach until you reach a beautiful **rock tower** (choice of route depends on tides!). Here you climb a grassy embankment and walk along sheep paths through partially swampy land, following the coastline until you come to a steep inlet. The sea birds, which nest in the cliffs, can be well observed from here. The three-toed seagull is the most common bird which breeds here. There are several hundred thousand breeding pairs of these birds in Iceland. From time to time, you can also see herring gulls and, often in the same swarm, the polar seagulls. Each of these species has only about 5000 breeding pairs. In addition, you have a good view of the colorful liparite cliffs further to the northeast.

The **return** is best if you walk somewhat above the edge of the cliffs, also along a sheep path.

While walking along the beach, you can also see this waterfall.

Northern Iceland
Akureyri – Jökulsárgljúfur National Park – Mývatn

View from Vindbelgjarfjall across the Mývatn region.

From Egilsstathir towards the west, the Ring Road leads you through vast, isolated areas. Only few roads lead to the interior of the island from here. Along the coast to Ásbyrgi, 300 km of mostly rough roads have to be overcome, but it is possible to do so by car. It is difficult to go further by bus in this region. The landscape offers beautiful views of the coast time and again such as the Melrakkaslétta Peninsula but this vast, treeless moorland is not suitable for hiking. The only detour we can recommend is the bird cliffs near Rauthinúpur.

The Jókusárgljúfur National Park was founded in 1973 and now stretches across 150 km². It runs from north to south along the Jökulsá á Fjöllum Glacial River, which continuously flows down mighty waterfalls, the Dettifoss being the most famous thereof. The overwhelming beauties of the park include the idyllic Vesturdalur with the imposing basalt formations of the Hljóthaklettar, the most colorful volcanic mountain in Iceland, the Rauthhólar and the green Hólmatungur Valley with its beautiful waterfalls. The climate in this region is, by Icelandic standards, rather dry (400 mm annual accumulation). Snow can still be present in May or June. With the bus line, you can reach the beginning of the national park, to Ásbyrgi, where two beautifully situated camping sites, a national park office (open from June 15 to September 1) and a shop with a cafeteria can be found. On the west bank of the

Jökulsá á Fjöllum, a slope passes Vesturdalur, Hólmatungur and Dettifoss and leads to the Ring Road. This is for the most part passable as far as Dettifoss. There is no public bus connection, but since many tourist busses and private vehicles travel this road, organizing a ride shouldn't present any problems.

Since 1974, the land surrounding Mývatn and the Laxá River has been a nature preserve. With a total area of 37 km², the Mývatn is among the largest inland bodies of water in Iceland. However, it is only 2.5 – 4.5 m deep. Its name, »Mosquito Lake«, comes from the swarms of mosquitoes which can be found there every summer and which are the main source of nutrition for birds and fish. All 15 species of ducks found in Iceland breed here. Fifty islands, many of which are so-called pseudo-craters, characterize the appearance of the lake. Because of its location on the western edge of an active volcanic zone, you can find more varying geological occurrences here than almost anywhere else. In addition, these are relatively easy to reach. In this region there are some 50 farmsteads today and the small village of Reykjahlith, which offers a supermarket, camping site, hotel, swimming pool, restaurant, bicycle rental, National Park Office and a small airport (from which it is possible to take highly recommended air tours of the region) and basically a good infrastructure. A good deal of the hikes can begin directly in the village, so it is no wonder that the Mývatn is one of the tourist centers of Iceland. But even here, you are spared the sight of swarms of tourists because there is only enough room for a half a dozen busses in front of the main »drive-in« tourist attractions. Those who want to obtain an extensive impression of this area should take at least 5 – 7 days time. There are daily bus connections between Akureyri and Egilsstathir and from here you can find numerous guided bus tours, for example to Askja.

As late as 1816, Akureyri was a settlement with only 45 inhabitants but grew to the third largest city in Iceland because of its good location and harbor. Located in the splendidly beautiful Eyjafjörthur, Akureyri is a good place to relax and go shopping and can also be a cosy place to await the passing of a bad weather front. It is surrounded by snow-covered mountains (also in summer), has many old, colorfully painted wooden houses, an interesting botanical garden and all attributes of a large Icelandic city. In the summer, the city is a good starting point for hikes and you can go on skiing and short-carving tours from May to June. Advantages are the daily bus connections to Reykjavik, Mývatn, Egilsstathir and Olafsfjörthus as well as air connections to many places in Iceland. Hotels, youth hostels and camping sites, which are ideally situated next to the beautiful newly constructed swimming pool but are unfortunately located next to a busy street, offer accommodations for everyone.

20 At the Rauthinúpur volcano

A short ascent to the volcano chimney with lively bird life

Núpskatla (farm) – lighthouse – Rauthinúpur

Location: Kópasker, 10 m.
Starting point: Núpskatla farm. From Route 85, a stretch of road branches off to the farm, be sure to close the gate! If you meet someone at the farm, be sure to ask for permission to park. Approach: Only by car on Route 85 or a guided tour.
Walking time: Total 1 hr.
Ascent: 70 m.
Grade: Don't go too close to the edge of the steep coast.
Accommodation: In Rópasker and Rafarhöfn.
Advice: Don't forget binoculars, a tripod and telephoto lens. July is better suited for observing the birds than August.

The bird-covered cliffs on the northwestern corner of the Melrakkaslétta Peninsula are a recommended detour for travellers who are interested in bird-watching. Seldom can the structure of a cliff full of sea birds be observed so well as here. Close to the water line, we find the green cormorant, above that on narrow rims the Atlantic murre and the Brunnich's guillemot, which breed very closely together, as well as the razor-billed auk in caverns and gaps. Rauthinúpur's cliffs are also one of eight breeding grounds for the Northern gannet in Iceland, the largest and most elegant sea bird of the island. The upper levels of the cliffs are populated by puffins.

At the **farm**, you go to the right and through a gate towards the narrow coastal strip. You have to climb over the **dam**, which is covered with huge stones and is rather difficult to climb, to the other side of the lagoon, which takes 15 min. From here, you can see the two black-red colored basalt towers which rise from the sea. Along the electricity lines, a clear path leads you through a pasture to a **lighthouse**. To the right of it, off the steep coast, the bird cliffs rise from the sea. It is also worth an extra 5 min to climb to the edge of the crater of the **Rauthinúpur** Volcano, which has been inactive for a long time and from where you can find a nice panoramic view.

Return taking the same route.

Northern gannet colony on the cliffs of Rauthinúpur.

21 The Eyjan island of rock

A walk to a viewing point over the Ásbyrgi

Camping site – viewing point – camping site

Location: Ásbyrgi, 20 m.
Starting point: The front camping site in Ásbyrgi. Approach: With a guided tour or with a car along Routes 85 and 864.
Walking time: Camping site – viewing point ¾ hr. Total time: 1½ hrs.
Ascent: 60 m.
Grade: The walk to the viewing point is well worth the time and trouble. Careful at the edge of the cliffs!
Accommodation: Two camping sites in the Ásbyrgi.

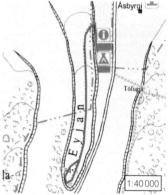

The Jökulsárgljúfur National Park stretches along the canyon of the Jökulsá á Fjöllum Glacial River. The camping site in the Ásbyrgi is an ideal starting point for tours. This short walk to the tip of the rock island offers a good opportunity to view the vegetation of the National Park. In preservation areas, mainly trees and bushes grow such as the birch, willow and mountain ash, but in contrast, the moorland only has dwarf bushes and lichen. Particularly on the rock island, you can find flowers like the cranesbill, angelica and bellflowers as well as the wintergreen, which is typical vegetation of the canyon. In all, approximately 220 higher species of plants can be found here because this region has a more continental climate than most of Iceland. Annual rain accumulation is 400 mm and the thermometer rises to an average 10°C in July. From the tip of the rock island, you have a beautiful view of the mighty formation of the **Ásbyrgi**, which, according to mythology, is the hoof print of Odin's horse. In reality, this »castle of the gods« (Ásbyrgi) is a part of the Jökulsá River Canyon which dried up a long time ago.

The marked trail begins directly behind the office of the **camping site**. It runs a bit out of the valley in order to lead you up the cliffs. From here, the trail goes south to the tip of the **rock island**. After a short loop, you follow the same trail back.

The Eyjan rock island in Ásbyrgi.

22 To Jökulsá canyon

Extensive circular hike from Ásbyrgi to the Jökulsá canyon

Ásbyrgi – Klappir – Jökulsárgljúfur – branch Áshöfthi – Ásbyrgi

Location: Ásbyrgi, 20 m.
Starting point: Front camping site in Ásbyrgi. Approach: With guided tours or with a car along Routes 85 and 864.
Walking time: Camping site – Klappir viewing point 1 hr; Klappir viewing point – Kviar Gorge 1 hr; along the canyon 1¼ hrs; to branch in Áshöfthi ¾ hr; Áshöfthi – camping site ¾ hr. Total time: 5 – 5½ hrs.
Ascent: 200 m.
Grade: Long hike with easy climbing along marked trails.
Accommodation: Camping site in Ásbyrgi.
Alternative route: At the branch in the trail, go further to the Áshöfthi rocks, from there north and the last part along the road back to the Ásbyrgi camping site. Additional ¾ – 1 hr.

This extensive tour from Ásbyrgi to the Jökulsá Gorge leads you to a viewing point from which you can see the impressive valley of the glacial river in its entirety. With its length of 25 km, width of 500 m and depth of up to 100 m, it is one of Iceland's mightiest canyons. It is located in the active volcanic zone and is therefore, geologically, still young.

The trail begins at the end of the front **camping site** and leads into and crosses the valley in an eastward direction towards the cliffs. Here the trail leads over the cliffs, which can be easily climbed, and there is a rope which adds additional help for the climb. At the signpost, stay to the right along the edge of the cliffs in the direction of **Vesturdalur**. From the **Klappir** viewing point (drawn too far to the south on the map), the trail leads you through an open moorland where only dwarf bushes and lichen can be found. The attentive and quiet hiker has an opportunity here to catch a view of the fauna

The Jökulsá has formed one of the broadest gorges in Iceland.

of this area. Most noticeable are the species of birds such as the golden plover, the white grouse, the pigeon hawk, the raven and several species of duck, but the arctic fox and mink can also be found here. After 1 hr, you will reach a **viewing point** with an orientation sign from which you have an impressive view of the **gorge**. Along the gorge there is a trail which we will follow to the north for 1 hr. Then the trail turns away from the canyon and runs through birch trees and after ¾ hr, we reach a fork in the trail on a meadow. The right trail takes us via **Áshöfthi** to Ásbyrgi. The Ás farm was one of the richest in Iceland but was destroyed by glacial currents in the 17th and 18th century. Straight ahead, we walk through cultivated land (meadows, pastures) back to **Ásbyrgi**. After 30 min, we reach the point of descent and are back at the **camping site** after only a few minutes.

23 Hljóthaklettar – Rauthhólar

To Iceland's most colorful volcano

Vesturdalur – Hljóthaklettar – Rauthólar and back

Location: Ásbyrgi, 20 m.
Starting point: Vesturdalur parking lot (reachable by car), 120 m. Approach: Route 862, which branches off Route 85 west of Ásbyrgi, is mainly passable by car to Dettifoss.
Walking time: Vesturdalur via Hljóthaklettar to Rauthhólar 1½ – 2 hrs; return 1 hr. Total time: 2½ – 3 hrs.
Ascent: 150 m.
Grade: Partially marked hiking tour on mostly wide and well-travelled trails.
Accommodation: Camping site Vesturdalur.
Alternative route: A short walk through Hljóthaklettar takes about 1 hr.

This extremely varied tour winds through the mighty volcanic funnel which was eroded away by the **Jökulsá á Fjöllum**. The basalt columns which often have a rosette form and which can be seen closely here were created by contractions and erosion during the cooling phase of the lava.
From the **camping site**, you follow the road 500 m to the parking lot, where the wide and marked trail begins. When the trail curves back to the left, you should go along this way for several meters to the imposing lava caverns but then go back to the main trail and hike further on the worn, clearly inclining path through the rock formations. From a small saddle, you can see the red foothill of the Rauthhólar Volcano rising behind a mighty basalt wall. You should branch off to the right and then again to the left and head towards a gap in the wall. Behind this, the trail inclines steeply and leads along a ridge on the foothill. The trail then goes further to the summit of the **Rauthhólar**, where you can enjoy the play of colors on the side of the volcano, which range from a reddish-yellow to black, as well as the panoramic view of the Jökulsá Gorge. The **return trip** follows along the marked trail which leads to the **parking lot** somewhat above (to the west) the rock formations.

Red colored slag gave Rauthhólar its name.

24 Hólmatungur

A walk to an idyllically located waterfall

Hólmatungur Parking lot – waterfall and back

Location: Ásbyrgi, 20 m.
Starting point: Hólmatungur parking lot (can just barely be reached by car). Approach: Route 862 (see Tour 23).
Walking time: Hólmatungur parking lot – waterfall 20 min; waterfall – parking lot ½ hr. Total time: 1 – 1¼ hrs.
Ascent: 80 m.
Grade: A nice walk, partially through a birch forest, down to a narrow pass in the Jökulsá gorge with a beautiful waterfall.
Accommodation: Vesturdalur camping site.
Alternative route: Go to the northwest along the gorge to Hólmarfossar and from there in a bend along the cliffs to the parking lot. 1½ – 2 hrs.

The Hólmatungur region has a rich vegetation considering its altitude (200 m above sea level). The trail takes us through a birch forest and at the springs and streams, plants grow which prefer a wet environment such as angelica (Angelica archangelica) and rare species of moss.

In front of the **parking lot**, a marked trail leads down to the **Jökulsá**. After 500 m, a trail branches off to the left but we go straight ahead in order to branch off after a further 500 m. We cross a bridge to the edge of the gorge where the path leads along a small bend. Here the Jökulsá forces its way through narrow passes (only a few meters wide) and plunges over smaller and larger waterfalls into the bubbly basins.

The **return trip** either leads us back the same way or along a long bend in the **Hólmarfossar** (see variations).

Tip for photographers: This area has good conditions for macro exposures of plants. Since the depth of focus dramatically decreases with close exposures, a tripod is absolutely necessary because of the small f-stops and long exposure times (unless you use a TTL flash, best with a cable for a more variable position). Those who can't afford an expensive macro lens can also use a close-up lens.

A branch of the Jökulsá.

25 Dettifoss

A walk to Europe's mightiest waterfall

Parking lot – Dettifoss – parking lot

Location: Ásbyrgi, 20 m.
Starting point: Parking lot at Dettifoss/Sanddalur (reachable by car). Approach: Route 862, as in Tours 23 and 24.
Walking time: ½ hr to Dettifoss.
Ascent: 40 m.
Grade: A short walk, be careful on the edge of the gorge because the stones and grass are slippery due to the mist, take along a raincoat.
Alternative route: You can go to Hafragilsfoss from Dettifoss (the slope to Hafragilsfoss cannot be reached by car) and then go along the Hafragil Gorge along a bend until you reach a slope which is first taken to the south and then followed left back to the parking lot. Approximately 2 – 3 hrs.

If you have gone to the trouble of driving along Route 862, it is recommended that you take the time to visit one of the main tourist attractions of Iceland, the Dettifoss, from the west side. The 30 kilometer long Jökulsá Canyon also begins here. Waterfalls developed along this canyon's fault lines which have carved their way through layers of basalt and can be seen at the beautiful basalt columns framing the Dettifoss. The Dettifoss, with a width of 100 m and a height of 45 m, is considered to be the most abundant waterfall in Europe (193 m³ of water every second).

From the parking lot, we follow the marked path eastward to the waterfall. The last part of the walk, which includes steps, is usually slippery because of the mist.

Advice: It is possible to combine the tours listed here (see variations) into a fascinating tour along the Jökulsá lasting several days. It is best to hitchhike to Dettifoss (or take an excursion bus) and then hike along the gorge to the camping site in Vesturdalur (6 – 7 hrs) and then further to Ásbyrgi (Vesturdalur – Ásbyrgi 4 – 5 hrs). By taking such a tour along the Jökulsá Canyon (which is up to 120 m deep), the hiker can get an impression of the varying landscape of this national park.

The Dettifoss is considered to be the most abundant waterfall in Europe.

26 Dimmuborgir

Through fascinating lava formations to the Hverfjall ash crater

Dimmuborgir – Jverfjall – Kirkja – Dimmuborgir

Location: Reykjahlith, 280 m.
Starting point: Dimmuborgir parking lot. Approach: By bus, car. Along Route 1.
Walking time: Parking lot – Hverfjall ¾ hr; Hverfjall – rock arch ½ hr; rock arch – long round tour (yellow marking) back to parking lot ¾ hr. Total time: 2 – 2½ hrs.
Ascent: 150 m.
Grade: Hike along marked trails, the Hverfjall is an ash crater and the ascent and descent are therefore dusty and »yielding«.
Accommodation: Hotel, camping at Reykjahlith.

Alternative routes: The points of departure for tours 26, 27 and 28 can be reached by bicycle (bicycle rental in Reykjahlith). The parts of Routes 848 and 1 around the lake are mostly paved, with detours the route is 40 km long and with the exception of the approach to Dimmuborgir, the gradients are not worth mentioning.

A connection to Tour 29 (Grjótagjá) is also possible on foot. You simply walk along the edge of the crater and descend on a path going north.

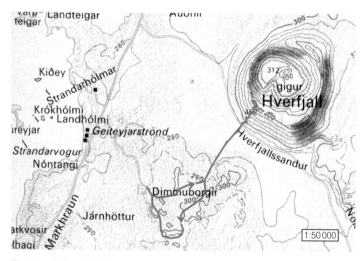

The Hverfjall, which is marked by a plateau covered with bizarre lava formations, was formed by a cold gas explosion. This can be noticed by the loose sand and gravel which form this crater. You should therefore not expect a view of a smoking crater gullet but the climb up the crater is worth the trouble for the panoramic view alone.

We can see Jverfjall through a lava arch.

Well-marked trails begin at the Dimmuborgir parking lot. We follow the red markings to **Hverfjall**. We reach the foot of this mountain through a lava arch. A zigzag trail makes the dusty ascent easier. Returning, you first go through the lava arch again and then follow yellow markers of the circular tour to **Kirkja** which lead to the left at a fork in the trail. The lava here has created an impressive portal. We pass many more formations which are suitable for the name **Dimmuborgir** (=Black Fortresses). After a full 2 hrs, we again reach our departure point.

27 Skútustathir

A walk along the green, »fake« crater at Mývatn

Skútustathir – starting point – Mývatn – Skútustathir

Location: Skútustathir, 260 m.
Starting point: Skútustathir, directly across from the cafeteria. Approach: By bus or car. Located on Route 1.
Walking time: ½ hr.
Ascent: 30 m.
Grade: Short walk.
Accommodation: In Skútustathir, Reykjahlith.
Alternative route: You can also detour and march back along the road, an additional ¾ hr. The short walk can also be well combined with a bicycle tour.

Pseudo-craters result from hot lava flowing over swampy areas. Steam and gasses then build these crater-like formations which can be found along the shores of the Mývatn. In July and August, this lake stands up to its name: the midges around this lake don't bite but a mosquito net to cover your head can be useful in order to avoid a snack with every breath you take. In the region of Laxá, biting mosquitoes can be found. For this reason, the Mývatn is of great interest mainly to ornithologists. Singing swans live here as well as common loons, grey geese, red throated divers, gerfalcons, pigeon hawks, meadow pipits, wagtails and redpolls among many other species. The crater, which is grown over by grass and moss, the lake and the hopefully blue sky create a charming motive.

Starting at the **cafeteria**, our trail begins across the road and leads us past several smaller craters to a viewing point. Here you have a view of the entire **lake**. The Vindbelgjarfjall rises to the north. From the viewing point, you go southwest through a meadow and back along the lake and the trail ends near the school in **Skútustathir**.

Advice: The pseudo-craters are most impressive from the air. If the weather is good, we recommend an air tour from Reykjahlith which, depending on the length of the tour, gives you a good view of all volcanic occurrences in the area as far as Askja.

The pseudo-crater near the Mývatn can easily be recognized.

28 Vindbelgjarfjall, 529 m

A short, steep ascent to a viewing point which is well worth the climb

Vagnbrekka – Vindbelgjarfjall summit and back

Location: Reykjahlith, 280 m.
Starting point: On Route 848, just before the Ring Road until shortly before the Vagnbrekka farm (in the direction of Reykjahlith), then 1 km along a deep trail. Approach: By bus, car; on Route 1.
Walking time: Ascent ½ hr; descent ¼ hr. Total time: ¾ – 1 hr.
Ascent: 260 m.
Grade: Steep, somewhat stony ascent with slippery gravel.
Accommodation: In Reykjahlith.
Alternative route: If you combine tours 26 – 28 into a cycling tour (see variations Tour 26), there is a direct approach possibility to the point of ascent.

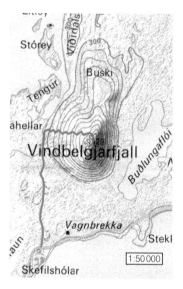

On a clear day, the panoramic view from Vindbelgjarfjall is unforgettable. From here, you can easily recognize the varying forms of the landscape which has been shaped by volcanoes. Table mountains like the Burfell were created by strong volcanic eruptions, tuff or palagonite crests like the Namafjall were created by smaller eruptions during the last Ice Age some 10,000 years ago when the entire region was covered by a glacier.

Shortly before the **Vagnbrekka** farm, a deeply rutted lane leads to the foot of the mountain. It is marked by white pegs and the 1 kilometer can easily be travelled by bicycle. The ascent is made along a steep but clearly visible path leading directly to the summit. In addition, the peg markings help with orientation. In order to protect the vegetation, you should not leave the path. Surprisingly quickly, you reach the **summit** after only 30 min.

The same path takes us back very quickly.

View across Mývatn from Vindbelgjarfjall.

29 Grjótagjá

A pleasant circular route to hot fissures

Reykjahlith – Stóragjá – Grjótagjá – gravel quarry – Reykjahlith

Location: Reykjahlith, 280 m.
Starting point: Junction of Route 1 and Route 87. Approach: By bus, car, located on Route 1.
Walking time: Center of town – Stóragjá ¼ hr, Stóragjá – Grjótagjá 1 hr; Grjótagjá – infusorial earth 20 min; infusorial earth – center 20 min. Total time: 2 hrs.
Ascent: 10 m.

Grade: An easy hike, also possible during bad weather conditions. No possibilities for swimming because the Stóragjá is supposed to have a high bacteria content and Grjótagjá is too hot (50 °C).
Accommodation: Hotel and camping site in Reykjahlith.
Alternative route: Detour to Hverfjall. From Grjótagjá take the trail to the south.

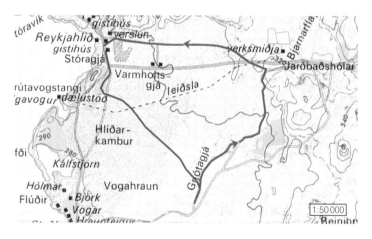

In the immediate vicinity of the town of Reykjahlith, interesting observations of nature can be made in a small area. The Vogahraun lava field displays increasing vegetation with crippled birch trees on its edge as well as ground plants such as the stemmless toadflax, saxifrage, thrifts and lichen. In addition, water-filled, hot gaps like the famous Grjótagjá can be found.

A path leads the way directly in front of the **junction**. Soon on the right side, you will find a deep trench (approximately 10 m deep). From here, wooden stairs lead down to the **Stóragjá Bathing Cavern**. Our trail then leads us up the trench. Soon you will find yourself in a birch forest with rather short trees, cross a heating pipe and you will then leave the forest again. This transitional

Plants like the stemless toadflax are slowly taking over the lava desert.

zone with crippled tree growth and flowers in black sand offers many photographic possibilities. Through this barren area of sand and lava, the trail leads us to a sustained gap, rises several meters and comes to a road which goes to Hverfjall. Warning signs show the way to the **Bathing Cavern**, which can be found in this rift. The water is in the process of cooling down, but in 1994, the temperature (50°C) was still much too hot to bathe in. We follow the lane to the north. Above all, the hills to the right are filled with many smaller gaps from which hot steam rises. The road then meets Route 1 directly across from the **infusorial earth** (the gravel is a sediment of gravel algae) with its noticeable blue lake. We walk along the main road for a while and then come to a secondary road which branches off to the right; we pass a swimming pool, and return to **Reykjahlith**.

30 A circular tour of a solfataric area

A circular tour between sulphur and mud holes

Námaskarth Pass – Hverarönd – Námafjall Summit – and back

Location: Reykjahlith, 280 m.
Starting point: When coming from Reykjahlith, you will see two distinguishable sulphur hilltops on the right shortly after the Námaskarth Pass and the viewing points and a trail. You can leave your car or bicycle here. Approach: By bus or car, on Route 1.
Walking time: Námaskarth Pass – Hverarönd ¼ hr; Hverarönd – Námafjall Summit ½ hr; Námafjall Summit – Pass ½ hr. Total time: 1¼ – 1½ hrs.
Ascent: 120 m.
Grade: The tour leads through the solfataric area, pay close attention to warning signs and barriers and stay on the path!
Accommodation: In Reykjahlith.
Alternative route: Tours 30 and 31 can be combined into a somewhat demanding bicycle tour. The distance between Reykjahlith and Krafla is 15 km, on the way there and back, there is an incline of a good 450 m to be overcome. You ride east along Route 1

(Egilsstathir) and across the Námafjall (20% inclination). About 1 km past the Námaskarth solfataric area, the street branches off to the left towards Krafla.
Advice: Due to acidic gasses, you should protect your lens with a UV filter.

The variety of colors in Námafjall as well as the smoking, hissing and bubbling sulphur and mud pits attract many tourists who usually disappear into an air-conditioned bus after a short visit. We will however hike further to the summit of the Námafjall, from where we will have a good view of the volcanic landscape laying before us. The various colors of Námafjall are caused by different minerals. The yellow is, for example, sulphuretted hydrogen, free sulphuric acid and sulphates, as well as varieties of algae which are suited for the hot water, which can reach temperatures of 100 °C.
From the **pass**, we go down the road to the Hverarönd hot spring area. The path takes us along a slope to the left past mud pits, solfataras and steaming springs. White peg markings lead us further to the **summit**. Shortly before the highest point, a road ends which we will follow to the north. On the right, the

sulphur hilltops which served for orientation purposes earlier will again appear. Sulphur used to be mined in this area. Shortly afterwards, we will again reach the **starting point** of this tour.

Boiling sulphur pit at the foot of the Námafjall.

31 Krafla

A spectacular circular tour through one of Iceland's youngest lava fields

Reykjahlith – Leirhnjúkur – Hófur and back

Location: Reykjahlith, 280 m.
Starting point: Above the Kröfluvirkjun Power Plant, there is a parking lot on the left after a steep part in the road. Approach: By bus or car. Side road from Route 1.
Walking time: 1 – 3 hrs.
Ascent: 50 m.
Grade: Active volcanic zone, solfataras, stay on the path!
Accommodation: In Reykjahlith.
Alternative routes: A different path also leads to Krafla from Reykjahlith but is 10 km long. For a cycling tour, you can easily combine tours 30 and 31 as well as a detour to the Viti Crater, which is some hundred meters above the Krafla parking lot.

The Krafla is a central volcano with a diameter of 20 km. Lava comes out of its mighty magma chambers to the surface through gaps which are caused by the continental drift. There have been several new eruptions here since 1975, the last occurring in 1984. Fresh black lava, smoking gaps and solfataras create a feeling that one is at the beginning of creation. Noisy groups of tourists can disrupt the sensitivity of nature, but on the other hand, because of these groups, a marked trail has been built just in the past few years. Photographers will be amazed at the wide variety of motives offered by a view from the Hófur Crater. A tour scheduled to last 1 hr can easily become a tour lasting 3 hrs.

A trail takes us from the **parking lot** straight to solfataras embedded in the slopes of the Leirhnjúkur. From this point, and after the second solfatara field, we go further to the right across the fresh lava of the last eruptions. The path here is a bright line and easy to recognize. We stay along the small crater of **Hófur**, the path leads us to its interior. From above, you have a good view of the volcanic zone with the layers of lava with varying ages (black = young, brown = older). Before the crater of the volcano, the path curves off and leads us to a smoking gap and along the back side of the Leirhnjúkur. In a bend to the left, the path runs into the path coming from Reykjahlith and leads us back to the main trail and to the **starting point**.

The young lava field of Krafla.

32 The Herthubreitharlindir oasis

Several tours around the only oasis in the Ódádahraun lava desert

1. Herthubreitharlindir – Ódádahraun and back
2. Herthubreitharlindir – Jökulsá á Fjöllum and back
3. Herthubreitharlindir – Álftavatn and back

Location: Reykjahlith, 280 m.
Starting point: Herthubreitharlindir cabin, some 500 m. Approach: By bus, car, plane; on Route 1 to Reykjahlith. From there bus connection to the starting point: From July 15 to August 15 daily, from June 20 to August 31 Mondays, Wednesdays and Fridays. Since the visit is very short on a guided tour, we recommend taking breaks (at no extra charge) and spending the night. Otherwise arrival possible with four-wheel drive vehicles.
Walking time: Circular tour through Ódádahraun (*green*) ¾ hr; circular tour to Jökulsá á Fjöllum (*orange*) 1½ hrs; to

Álftavatn 1½ hrs (*red*).
Ascent: 10 m.
Grade: Marked trail without problems.
Accommodation: Camping site near the Akureyri Touring Club cabin, in the summer a caretaker is present.
Alternative route: From here, the yellow markers lead to the only (considerable) ascent to the Herthubreith, 7 hrs to the summit, ascent dangerous because of falling stones. Less recommendable is the hike to the cabin near Braethrafell. From there, there is a path leading south to Askja, mostly unmarked, extremely long (29 km and 15 km) with difficult daily stages.

In the middle of the Ódádahraun Lava Desert, the place where outlaws hid with only little chance of surviving, the Herthubreith rises, a table mountain made of hyaloklastite, that is of magma which has been fossilized beneath glacial ice. If you go by bus to the »Outlaw's Desert« and spin along the expansive landscape free of vegetation and water, you will be more than

The cabin near Herthubreith is the starting point of these hikes.

surprised when the bus reaches the green oasis at Herthubreitharlindir. At the foot of the »Queen of Icelandic Mountains«, three walking tours offer a good opportunity to become acquainted with this area.

The green markings lead (¾ hr) through the **Ódádahraun** Lava Field past the rocky pit where the outlaw Fjalla-Eyvindur hid in the winter of 1774/75. He survived without fire, eating only roots and horsemeat.

The orange colored marking leads to **Jökulsá á Fjöllum** (1½ hrs), which forcibly carved its way through the lava.

The red markings lead to **Àlftavatn** (1½ hrs), where singing swans can often be observed.

33 To Öskjuvatn

A short walk through the impressive Caldera of Askja

Parking lot – Vitilaug – Öskjuvatn and back

Location: Reykjahlith, 280 m.
Starting point: End of the road to Askja (depending on snow), parking lot. Approach: By bus, car, plane; along Route 1 to Reykjahlith. From there bus connections to starting point. From July 15 to August 15 daily, from June 20 to August 31 Mondays, Wednesdays and Fridays. The bus tour can be interrupted without paying extra. Otherwise only reachable with a four-wheel drive vehicle.
Walking time: ½ – ¾ hr in each direction, in total 1½ – 2 hrs.
Ascent: 50 m.
Accommodation: The Akureyri Touring Clubs Dreki cabin, be sure to reserve in advance, and a camping site 8 km before the Askja parking lot.
Alternative route: A nice walk into the Drekagil Gorge from the Dreki cabin. The gorge is filled with bizarre lava forms and a waterfall at the end (in all ¾ hr).

The mighty massive Dyngjufjöll Volcano, which is 1,500 m high, with the fascinating 50 km² Askja Caldera, looks like a moon landscape and NASA astronauts actually prepared for their moon landing here. Dyngjufjöll is the remainder of a strato-volcano. To the southeast of its Caldera is the Öskjuvatn, which was blocked in by streams of lava in 1921 and 1930. The last major eruption, an eruption along its gaps, was in 1961, which is shown by the Vikrahaun Lava Field, through which the road runs.

Those who are able to reach this area with a recreational vehicle or touring bus only need a little luck with the weather because, although there is relatively little annual accumulation, the weather is often stormy and cold due to the elevation and snow storms are possible.

The trail leads us from the **parking lot**, slightly inclining, across a small saddle and through blackish-red slag along marking posts to the large **Öskjuvatn**. Along the way, you will pass the **Vitilaug** Crater Lake, which is commonly called »Hell« not only because of its sulphuric smell. In 1875, mighty amounts of pumice stone and ashes shot out of this crater, reaching as far as Stockholm, and transformed vast regions in northern Iceland into deserts. The milky-white sulphuric water has a temperature of approximately 28°C and is an inviting place to bathe for those who can't smell. The descent into the crater is very slippery when it rains. The walls of the crater are brightly colored by minerals. A short walk later and you will reach the shore of the lake. Here you can find large pumice stones which are so light that they float on the water. The small volcanic island Eyja rises in the middle of the lake. We take the same trail back to the **starting point**.

The Caldera of Askja with Öskjuvatn and Viti as seen from an airplane.

34 Súlur, 1213 m

An ascent to the mountain viewing point of Akureyri

Akureyri – Súlurvegur – Súlur and back

Location: Akureyri (harbor town).
Starting point: Along Súlurvegur, on the right shortly before the waste dump, there is a parking lot after some 250 m (a good 3 km from the center). Approach: By plane or with the bus or car on Route 1.
Walking time: Parking lot – summit 2½ hrs; summit – parking lot 1¾ hrs. Total time: 4¼ – 4½ hrs.
Ascent: 1000 m.
Grade: The trail is only scarcely marked with posts and depending on the time of year runs more or less across fields of snow, the edges of which can be swampy.
Accommodation: In Akureyri.
Alternative route: Nice skiing and short-carving tours in the spring.

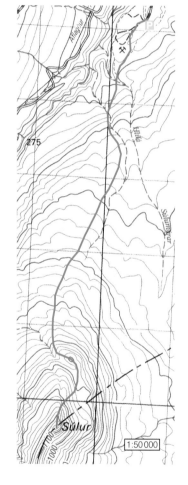

The Súlur rises strikingly above Akureyri and appears so close that you could touch it. The greatest hurdle in reaching its summit is the road leading to the starting point of the tour. Without your own vehicle, the tour takes an extra 1½ – 2 hrs.

From here, the initially well-seen path marked with posts goes continuously towards the summit. It first leads us along the ridge of a hill and then along this ridge across some steps. More than anything else, the hills of the Thúfur meadow make walking strenuous. The fields of snow in the higher parts of the Súlur, which remain until the summer, prevent the construction of a clear path. Post markings can also no longer be found here. The further course is sufficiently characterized by »straight ahead and uphill«. In a flat hollow at the latest, you should cross from the left ridge to the main ridge and climb this one. A clear path can be found here. The fields of snow are not particularly steep and can easily be climbed with good mountain boots. At the **summit**, marked by a pile of stone, you have a panoramic view of the snow-covered mountains of Akureyri and Eyjaförthur. It could be worth taking along a stable nylon bag for the descent so that you can slide down the fields of snow.

The trail leads across Thúfur meadow to Súlur.

35 Dalvík – Olafsfjörthur

This long hiking tour follows an old connecting trail

Dalvík – Karlsárdalur – Bustarbrekkudalur – Olafsfjörthur

Location: Olafsfjörthur, 20 m.
Starting point: Shortly past Dalvík (in the direction of Olafsfjörthur) there is a parking lot near the abandoned Karlsa farm (with a new house next to it) with a memorial stone. Approach: By car or bus. From Monday to Friday, there is a bus connection from Olafsfjörthur to Dalvík departing at 8.30.
Walking time: Parking lot – electric poles and hedgerow 2 hrs; electric poles and hedgerow – ridge 1 hr; ridge – lake 1¼ hr; lake – Olafsfjörthur ¾ hr. Total time: 5 –

5½ hrs.
Ascent: 950 m.
Grade: In both valleys, a lane and the electric poles show the direction, but the ascent and descent of the ridge is unmarked and there is no trail (fields of snow) and therefore only possible when the weather is good. In the Vustarbrekku Valley, a wild stream has to be forded.
Accommodation: Free camping site near the swimming pool or Hotel in Olafsfjörthur.

From the **parking lot**, we go up the left side of the valley to **Karlsárdalur**, first towards the electric poles and then following them. After ½ hr, we come to a first steep incline of 200 m but then it is flat again. We follow the lane further until we cross a stream after a further ¾ hr. At this point, the lane is rather shabby and muddy. After a total of 2 hrs, the electrical line bends to the right and leads up a steep ridge. The lane also ends here.

View of Bustarbrekkudalur.

A further ascent and descent along the electric poles is safer for orientation, but the fields of snow are dangerously steep! Therefore it is better for us to go straight ahead on the right side of the slope to the end of the valley and then climb up the field of snow and keep to the right. We reach the ridge after a total of 3 hrs. From there we have a magnificent view of the surrounding mountains and as far as the fjords. It is important to descend into the **Bustarbekkudalur Valley** from here, where the electric poles continue. We orient ourselves towards the lake (not along the lane next to the electric poles!). First a field of

snow offers us a quick »descent« and then we go along the left side of the slope, where rubble and swampy spots make walking to the lake unpleasant. After 1¼ hrs, we reach the lake. From here, we can proceed without problems along the trail.

We climb steps and can already see the end of the valley. Near the water pipe house, you should look for a possibility to ford the stream and then the lane leads us along the right slope down to the village. The lane which goes straight ahead spares us from fording the stream but leads us directly through a farm where there are unfriendly Saint Bernard dogs. After 5½ hrs, we reach **Olafsfjörthur** where the beautiful new swimming pool and above all the hot water spring are the perfect conclusion of this tour.

36 Kotágil gorge

Canyoning to a surprising waterfall

Parking lot – gorge – waterfall and back

Location: Akureyri.
Starting point: On the Ring Road Route 1, approximately 7 km before Silfrastathir (coming from Akureyri). Directly before the bridge over the Kotá, there is a possibility to park on the right side. Approach: By car or bus (only once daily).
Walking time: ½ hr in each direction.
Ascent: 20 m.
Grade: Narrow path, the stream has to be crossed at least twice, rubber boots that reach to the knee keep your feet dry.
Accommodation: In Akureyri.
Advice: The tour into the deep Kotágil is only recommended for tourists with their own vehicle.

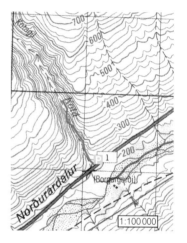

Between Akureyri and the small settlement of Varmahlíth, the Ring Road leads through the almost unpopulated Öxnadalsheithi region, which is surrounded by 1000 m high, steep mountains.

From the **parking lot**, we climb down the banks of the stream near the old bridge and enter the **gorge**, which has impressive colors and rock formations. Soon the slopes tower high and steep. They gain 500 m altitude in a stretch of only 3 kilometers. After three bends, the trail goes up a cliff (if the water is low, you can also walk along the banks). After several further bends, a rock wall on the right blocks the dry trail and the stream has to be crossed to the left. Here you can already hear the roaring of the water. Shortly thereafter you have to cross again to the right and suddenly you will be standing in front a beautiful waterfall.

Take the same trail back.

Advice: If the gorge should be flooded, you can climb along its right side and have a cautious view of it in places.

The entrance to the Kotágil Gorge.

Western Iceland
Vatsnes peninsula – Western fjords – Snaefellsnes – Reykjavik

The Vatnsnes Peninsula, which can only be reached by private vehicle, magically attracts animal lovers. The best place in Iceland to watch seals is the Hindisvík Nature Preserve. The Western Fjords are geologically the oldest part of Iceland. The masses of land jut out into the Northern Atlantic like fingers, separated by the numerous fjords. Their exposed position is noticeable when you first look at a map and here you can count on bad weather conditions and constantly changing weather more often than in any other region of Iceland.

Isafjörthur, the largest city in the Western Fjords, can only be reached quickly by plane. With a bus or car you need a long time because the distances along the fjords are long. In Isafjörthur, you can also find a tourist information office which offers current information and can arrange for local guides (Fjorthungssamband Vestfirthinga, Athalstraeti 7, P.O. box 277, 400 Isafjörthur, Tel. 00354 456 5121 (4780), Fax 00354 456 5185 (3508)).

The central part of the Western Fjords is mostly a tundra landscape, whipped by the wind, which is covered by many small lakes and streams. The climax of every adventure into the Western Fjords is certainly the steep coast (cliffs) of Látrabjarg, the westernmost point not only of Iceland but also of Europe. Here you can get within a few steps of the puffins.

From the Western Fjords, you can reach the Snaefellsnes Peninsula easily with the ferry. When the weather is nice, you can catch a glimpse of the bright white glacier at Snaefellsjökull from afar. The magnificently beautiful conical central volcano with a height of 1446 m is not only characterized by its imposing looks but also by its role in literature. Jules Vernes placed the entrance to the center of the earth at this point. The entire peninsula, which is considered to be a »Miniature Iceland«, offers numerous geological and ornithological peculiarities, beginning with the lava fields (Berserkjahraun) and volcanic craters to extremely impressive coastal cliffs (Arnarstapi) with bird cliffs and the most beautiful sandy beach in Iceland as well as hidden and unexpected tuff formations. In order to travel around the peninsula, a vehicle is necessary which is capable of going up a slope near a glacier. There are only bus connections to Stykkishólmur and Hellisandur (Olafsvik). If you are inexperienced, we can only advise against climbing a glacier. The necessary equipment is important because of numerous glacial gaps. (Skiing tours are possible.) The Snaefells Peninsula can also be quickly reached from Reykjavik.

More than 150,000 people live in the Reykjavik metropolitan region. The northernmost capital in the world presents itself as a modern, growing city

The Gullfoss, the »golden waterfall«, is a frequently visited site.

with two harbors, a bus station and the largest domestic airport in Iceland. The center, with its pedestrian zone around the main post office and the surrounding business district are very inviting and of course, you can also buy good wool products here (sales around the end of August). The large »Kringlan« shopping center is on the outskirts of town.

Of course there are hotels here, a youth hostel (book in advance!) and a camping site (a beautiful, well-managed site near the swimming pool where you can also find valuable information).

37 Vatnsnes peninsula

A walk to the seals of Hindisvík

Hindisvík – left side of the bay – cliffs and back

Location: Hvammstangi, 40 m.
Starting point: At the northern point, there is the abandoned Hindisvík farm in the nature preserve of the same name. In front of the farm, you can find a small parking place. Approach: By car along Route 711.
Walking time: ½ hr each direction.
Ascent: 10 m.
Grade: Walk.
Accommodation: In Blönduós (hotel, camping, youth hostel) and in Hvammstangi (camping).
Advice: Don't forget binoculars and telephoto lens.

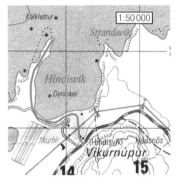

Although practically half of the world's population of the common seal (Phoca vitulina) lives around Iceland with a population of some 30,000, it isn't so easy to find these animals, which can be recognized by their round heads.

Seals lay lazily on the rocks.

The abandoned Hindisvík farm.

You have particularly good chances of seeing them at Hindisvík. In addition to the seals, you can also find many gray seals on these rocks. They become some 3 m long and have dark spots.

From the abandoned **Hindisvík farm**, a path with wooden steps leads you over the fence and then along a trail to an old building. From here, you go along the bay on the left side. A path leads you further towards some **rocks** in the sea. There you can observe the seals with binoculars. They also sometimes swim by and look curiously out of the water.

You take the same way back.

Advice: If you drive along Route 711 to the eastern coast of the Vatnsnes Peninsula towards the northern tip, you should definitely visit the sombre Borgarvirki basalt fortress and the Hvítserkur rocks which lay in the sea before you go further to the Hindisvík Nature Preserve.

38 Kaldalón

Across moraines to the hanging edge of a glacier

Kaldalón Bay – glacial arch – Kaldalón Bay

Location: Isafjörthur, 20 m.
Starting point: Kaldalón Bay. Before the bridge on the right side follow a small road to the edge of the moraines, the nature preserve begins here. Approach: You reach the Kaldalón Bay along Route 635, a bad road but it can be driven with a car.
Walking time: 1½ hrs per direction.

Ascent: 50 m.
Grade: Several streams which are not too deep have to be crossed or forded. Be careful when climbing the field of snow. The weather here can be very rough – Kaldalón means »Cold Lagoon«.
Accommodation: None.

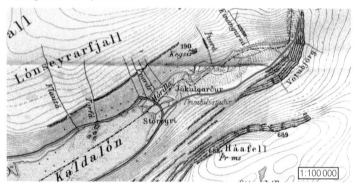

The Drangajökull plateau glacier, which rises 925 m, has an area of 160 km² in spite of strong shrinkage and still predominates the completely unpopulated part of the Western Fjords. In this lonely, majestic landscape, our tour leads us through a flat glacial valley between the sides of 600 m high mountains.

At the edge of the moraine, keep to the right along a lane which becomes a path. In the beginning, this can be seen well and leads across the moraines and hills of rubble. It then becomes difficult to recognize and the numerous way marks don't help. It is best if you keep to the right edge of the valley where there are many smaller streams to cross, all of which you can jump across. After a full hour, you will reach a red streambed. Here you climb up the field of snow on the right side. From there you will have a good view of the **glacial arch**, the waterfalls and the edge of the shrunken Drangajökull Glacier. You take the same trail back.

In front of the edge of the Drangajökull Glacier.

39 Dynjandifoss (Fjallfoss)

A walk along the most beautiful waterfall in the Western Fjords

Parking lot – path left or right of the waterfall and back

Location: Thingeyri, 20 m.
Starting point: Small parking lot at the foot of the waterfall. Approach: By car on Route 60.
Walking time: ½ hr to walk up either side, 20 min back.
Ascent: 60 m twice.
Grade: Walk.
Accommodation: Camping site at the foot of the waterfall.

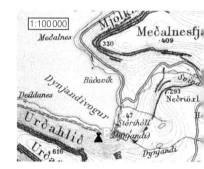

The Dynjandifoss is one of the most beautiful and impressive places in the Western Fjords and one of the most impressive waterfalls in Iceland. The entire area (some 700 hectares) has been a preserve since 1986. From the **parking lot**, the trail goes up the left side of the waterfall.

The river falls in several stages which results in many beautiful views of smaller waterfalls until you find yourself at the foot of the wide and majestic **Dynjandifoss**, which falls a good 100 m from the plateau. A path also rises on the right side of the waterfall, and it's worth climbing the falls again here where you can find a better view of some of the waterfalls. These five lower waterfalls are called Baejarfoss, Hundafoss, Göngufoss, Úthafoss and Háifoss. Fording below the Dynjandifoss is very dangerous because of the steep current.

You should go back to the **starting point** taking the same trail you climbed on.

Photographic tip: Here at the Dynjandifoss, you can find a wide range of photo motives ranging from details like the many types of moss to the wide, grandiose landscape. If you want to obtain a misty view of the waterfall, exposure times of more than one second and a stable tripod which can be used at eye-level as well as placed on the ground are necessary (without extension or inversion of the middle column). We recommend a tripod which can be spread variably (e.g. from Manfrotto and Gitzo). A pole filter also has an effect when the sky is cloudy, above all it results in fuller shades of green.

In several stages, the Dynjandi falls from the plateau into the fjord.

40 The fossils in Surtarbrandsgil

A simple hike to an interesting coal seam

Brjánslaekur – Laekjará Valley – Surtarbrandsgil – Brjánslaekur

Location: Brjánslaekur, 30 m.
Starting point: Shortly before the restaurant/café near the »Nature Preserve« sign.
Approach: Ferry from Stykkisholmuir, with the car on Route 60/62.
Walking time: ¾ hr in each direction. Total time: 1½ hrs.
Ascent: 50 m.
Grade: Short hike.
Accommodation: In Brjánslaekur.

The Surtarbrandsgil, named after for the fire giant Surtur, offers a unique opportunity to catch a glimpse of the vegetation of the tertiary of Iceland. The leaves of alders, poplars, birches, needles of pines, spruces, firs, and also of sequoias, which have established themselves with all detail in the crust of gravel algae, show a close relationship to the vegetation of North America today.

From the **sign**, we follow a lane which curves to the right towards a fence. We come to another fence and go through the (hopefully) open area to the left, where we follow the right bank of a stream. After ½ hr, you will see three rifts. The rift furthest to the right is the **Surtarbrandsgil Valley**. This valley runs some hundred meters to a small waterfall. From the left side of the valley, a scree slope goes down. Here you can find beautiful fossilized leaves which have been dated at approximately 11 million years. You can clearly recognize the various layers formed by deposits from rivers and volcanic eruptions (basalt and tuff). The many individual layers also contain different groups of fossils. It is typical of many fossils that the covering plate is covered with a light colored crust whereas the dark, coaled substance of the plant is found on the bottom plate. Since this is a nature preserve, please ask in the café if you are allowed to take one (!) piece along with you.

We go back the same way we came.

In the layers of coal in the gorge, we can find beautiful fossilized leaves.

41 Látrabjarg

A hike along the cliffs at Europe's westernmost point

Parking lot – cliff path – parking lot

Location: Patreksfjörthur, 20 m.
Starting point: Bjargtangar lighthouse (parking lot). Approach: By car on the (bad) Route 612.
Walking time: 1 – 2 hrs or longer if desired.
Ascent: 100 – 400 m.
Grade: Short walk or longer hike, both are possible along the steep coast. Caution, the edges of the cliffs are unstable, danger of collapsing!
Accommodation: In Breithavik, shortly before Látrabjarg, there is a simple but beautiful camping site directly on the ocean.

A large part of the 6 million puffins (Fratercula arctica arctica) in Iceland breeds along the Látrabjarg cliffs. These birds, which are about 30 cm long, have a wingspan of up to 63 cm. They can fly at a speed of up to 80 km / hr

Millions of puffins breed on the Látrabjarg cliffs.

Sunset at Europe's westernmost point.

and dive up to 60 m. After courting in April, the pairs look for their nesting grounds where they will spend the next three months breeding and raising their young in deep nesting caverns. Afterwards, the young animals spend 3 years alone at sea. The Icelanders still hunt these comical birds (which they have given the nickname »Provost«) without endangering the species.

The fascinating 14 km long coastal cliffs rise up to 450 m above the stormy sea and are one of the most important breeding grounds for sea birds in Iceland. July is therefore the best time to visit. Directly next to the lighthouse, the puffins sit on the edge of the cliffs and are not disturbed in the least by tourists. Masses of seagulls, guillemots and razor-billed auks can be found here. Kilometers of well-used paths lead across the cliffs, from which you always have new views of the birds and the mighty steep coast. How far you can go depends above all on the god of weather, who often sends storms and fog.

42 Berserkjahraun – Hraunsfjartharvatn

A circular tour from the Berserk Desert to the »Dragon Rocks«

Selvallavatn – Waterfall – Tuff Rock Formations – Viewing point and back

Location: Stykkishólmur, 40 m.
Starting point: First along route 56 from Stykkishólmur, then on Route 57 in the direction of Grundarfjörthur. 1 km after Route 56 branches off from Route 57 in the direction of Grundarfjörthur, follow an unpaved slope towards Berserkjahraun and reach the Selvallavatn Lake after 1 km.
Approach: Bus connection from Stykkishólmur to Olafsvík; Route 57.
Walking time: Lake – small waterfall ½ hr; small waterfall – ridge (horn) 1 hr; ridge – gorge ½ hr; gorge – lake 1 hr. Total time: 3 hrs.
Ascent: 230 m.
Grade: No markings, partially unclear path, only sheep paths, ascent of the tuff crest

steep in some places.
Accommodation: In Stykkishólmur.
Alternative route: Take the bend to Hraunsfjartharvatn, 1 ½ – 2 hrs longer.

The bizarre tuff formations below the Hraunsfjartharvatn were one of the most beautiful new discoveries of our last trip to Iceland. The small **Selvallavatn**, surrounded by lava fields and red volcanic craters, is an enchanting starting point for this hike.

On the left shore of the lake, we first go along a lane, a power line runs along the left. There are several smaller streams to cross and then the lane curves to the right. We still hike along the shore and have to cross a further stream (has to be forded at times) with a small **waterfall**. The lane ends and turns into a sheep path which runs to the west along the foot of the mountain. Swampy places and many mosquitoes lurk directly along the shore of the lake. We go along the contour line through a gorge which has been washed out and we continue along a shoulder in a second gorge and go up the left bank of the stream. Above, you recognize an expanse of tuff with a striking tower, which you will walk towards. Most fascinating are the **formations of rhyolithic tuff** to the right side of the tower, but there are several sloping spots which can only be conquered when the tuff is dry and bright. Below on the right, the path is marked by the stream. Where this valley ends, it is best if we climb over a field of rubble. At the crest of the **Horn** Hill, we first keep to the east across several smaller trenches and then go south towards the Hraunsfjartharvatn. To the left, the power line runs through a valley. After ½ hr, a trench offers us a possibility to turn and, if possible, to stay on the sheep path in order to protect the sensitive vegetation. A path along the power line leads us back to the **starting point**.

Bizarre tuff formations offer various motives.

43 Arnarstapi

A walk along a spectacular coast of cliffs

Monument – rock arch – harbor and back

Location: Arnarstapi, 40 m.
Starting point: Arnarstapi, parking lot at the monument. Approach: By car on Route 574.
Walking time: ¾ hr.
Ascent: 20 m.
Grade: Walk along the coast, watch out for the large holes in the rocks in the middle of the meadow.
Accommodation: Camping site in Arnarstapi, mattresses available, hotel in Búthir (20 km).
Alternative route: Guided tours of Snaefellsjökull are offered in Arnarstapi. This glacier is more dangerous than it looks because of its many gaps which are covered with snow, also in summer.

At the foot of Snaefellsjökull, the tide of the sea has uncovered volcanic chimneys, the lava of which has been solidified into a hexagonal shape in the form of pillars, caves and arches which provide ideal conditions for colonies of sea birds. The coastal sea swallows, three-toed seagulls and fulmars can especially be well observed here on smaller basalt islands in addition to many cormorants.

From the **parking lot**, a path takes us towards the coast. A fence must be crossed over a wooden bridge. After several minutes, you will be on the rock coast (which can suddenly break away) and will have an imposing view of the **rock arch**. The structures of the basalt make this even more impressive. From here, it's worthwhile to go along the coastline to the northeast. You will pass by a small pond where sea birds can often be found. The vertically falling rock holes with a connection to the sea are most impressive. These offer an ideal nesting spot for the shrieking colonies of seagulls. After ½ hr, you will reach the small **harbor**. There you can also find several rock towers and beautiful basalt formations.

Either take the same path back or go from the harbor along the street back to the **parking lot**.

The basalt arch »Gatklettur« near Arnarstapi.

116

44 Eldborg

Simple hike to the »Fire Castle« volcanic crater

Snorrastathir – crater and back

Location: Borgarnes, 30 m.
Starting point: Snorrastathir farm.
Approach: Bus connection along Route 54; arrival by car recommended: From Route 54, a secondary road which leads to the Snorrastathir farm branches to the left.
Walking time: 1 hr each direction.
Ascent: 70 m.
Grade: Short hike on a well-recognized path.
Accommodation: Borgarnes (hotel, camping).

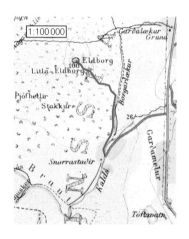

From the highest point in Eldborg, which originated around 900 A.D., you have an impressive view of the circular crater with its steeply rising walls. This crater is rightfully named the »Fire Castle«.

At the **Snorrastathir** farm, you will find an information sign after the bridge over the Kaldá. The path leads through an arch along the banks of a stream. After some 10 min, it curves to the left and goes towards the **Eldborg** (which can already be seen). The trail leads us zigzag through the Eldborghraun, which can otherwise hardly be crossed. The lava plate is at least 1000 years old and is covered with thick vegetation. The dwarf birches which have established themselves between the blocks of lava offer protection to many birds and the blueberries, bog bilberries and crowberries between the birches offer them food. After ¾ hr, you will reach the foot of the crater. Climbing it is not difficult but the rocks and above all the edge of the crater are very brittle. You take the same path back to the starting point.

Advice: If you drive along Route 54 some 10 km further to the northwest, you will reach a crossing. To the left, Route 767 leads further to Kolvitharnes where you can find a swimming pool. After a few kilometers the road to the right leads to the Gerthuberg farm where an imposing wall of beautifully formed basalt columns rises. The road leads further to Höfthi where you can find a large mineral spring.

The field of lava leading to the crater is thickly vegetated.

45 Hraunfossar

A walk along waterfalls coming from fields of lava

Parking lot – Barnafoss – Hraunfossar

Location: Húsafell, 150 m.
Starting point: Parking lot on Barnafoss.
Approach: Bus connection from Borgarnes to Húsafell via Reykholt and Munatharnes on Fridays and Sundays. By car on Route 519.
Walking time: ½ hr each direction.
Ascent: 20 m.
Grade: Walk, don't go too close to the glacial river!
Accommodation: Húsafell, camping site.
Alternative route: From Barnafoss to the Húsafell holiday settlement, 5 km partially along the road.

The **Barnafoss**, a beautiful waterfall, is only several dozen meters away from the **parking lot** and a well-built path leads you there. Two peasant children are supposed to have fallen from the natural stone bridge and the name (Children's Waterfall) comes from this tragic incident. However, the true attraction and feature are the **Hraunfossar**, the »Lava Waterfalls«. Along the banks across from the street a porous lava field stretches, the Hallmundarhraun. This descended from the Langjökull some 1200 years ago. Below this is a layer of ignimbrite (melted tuff from volcanic ash), which is impermeable and which prevents further seeping away from rainwater or melting water. This is a phenomenon which has created a row of waterfalls with a length of 1.5 km since the Hvítá River has carved the boarder between these layers of stone. You should not only watch this spectacle from the parking lot but also walk along a path on the banks. The many new and beautiful views of the numerous smaller waterfalls make this walk more than worthwhile!
Advice: If you are travelling with your own car, you can go some 5 km to the north of Húsafell to the Kalmannstunga (signs) farm and turn towards a slope which can be driven with normal cars until there is a place where you can turn around. Here you will find signs which direct you to the entrance to the lava caves Surtshellir (only for experienced climbers, ropes are necessary) and Ishellir. Entering it is not quite safe because of the iced entrance.

Numerous waterfalls fall from the moss-covered lava field.

46 Glymur

A demanding circular tour around Iceland's highest waterfall

Storibotn – ford – viewing point – Storibotn

Location: Botnsskáli, 40 m, on the old Ring Road at the end of the Hvalfjörthur.
Starting point: At the end of the fjord after the bridge, keep right and then turn left into a side road to Storbotn (2.5 km; parking lot).
Approach: Bus connection only on Saturdays after pre-booking.
Walking time: 1¾ hrs ascent, 1½ hrs de-

scent. Total time: 3¼ hrs.
Ascent: 250 – 300 m.
Grade: There is a ford above the waterfall, the descent along the edge of the gorge is partially exposed.
Alternative route: Along the side path back to the starting point, ½ hr.

The hike to the highest waterfall in Iceland leads from the 2000 hectare large Storibotn Nature Preserve, which is pleasant because of the high birch vegetation and the variety of flowers, to the barren higher plateau through which the Botnsá winds on the edge of the Hvalfell before it drops 200 m into the narrow gorge.

From the **parking lot**, go to the left across an iron bridge and then partially through the birch undergrowth on the left slope along a path which leads uphill. The path comes closer to the edge of the gorge and then curves left and leads you up a short field of rubble (don't pay attention to the way marks further on the left!). After the ascent, a flat part leads you further to a jeep path from where the relatively shallow but wide Botnsá River has to be forded (never during a flood, strong currents!). On the opposite bank, you first have to walk through a short swampy area. A path leads along the slope towards the south past the edge of the ravine along the **gorge**. On this path, you will come across three **viewing points** facing the gorge. You can best see the waterfall, which drops 200 m, and the narrow gorge, which is overgrown by green moss, from the third viewing point, which is a striking rock. At the end of the gorge, a steep path branches off to the right and leads you back down to the river (bridge). You hike back along the slope on the opposite side. The path along the river and over a shoulder is now narrower and leads you through small side-ridges. On one occasion a stream has to be jumped across. Afterwards, to the left above the path, a broad road can be seen which leads you over a bridge and past an abandoned farm back to the **parking lot**.

Iceland's highest waterfall drops 200 m into a narrow gorge.

Thingvellir

A simple circular tour at the most sacred place in Iceland

Hotel Valhöll – Öxaráfoss – Skógarkot – hotel

Location: Reykjavik, 30 m.
Starting point: Hotel Valhöll, parking opportunity. Approach: Bus connection to Reykjavik once daily; by car on Route 36.
Walking time: Hotel – Öxaráfoss ½ hr; Öxaráfoss – Skógarkot ¾ hr; Skógarkot – road ½ hr; road – hotel ¼ hr. Total time: 2 – 2½ hrs without detours.
Ascent: 30 m.

Grade: Diversified hike along a marked trail.
Accommodation: Hotel Valhöll, three camping sites in the national park.
Advice: In the hotel you can drink a coffee in style but for those who are trying to avoid calories, the delicious afternoon buffet with cakes, pies, rolls and as much coffee as you want should be avoided (around 10 US Dollars).

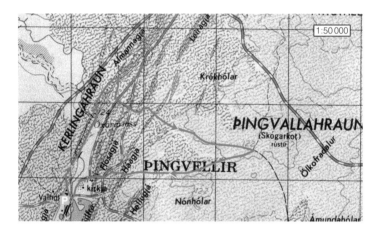

A path on the right near the hotel leads you partially across lava into the Allmannagjá gorge. This gorge is not only geologically interesting (it is the largest fault in this region), but also historically as the earlier meeting place of the Icelandic parliament.

We hike on a wide trail along the gorge, past the **Lögberg**, which is crowned with a flagpole. This is where laws were earlier read. Across a bridge and past the parking lot, we soon come to the **Öxarárfoss**. You can see this waterfall best from the path which branches off to the left and leads you across lava to an edge. Approximately 200 m further near a noticeable rock tower on the left, a path leads up a rock island where you have a good view of the Allmannagjá gorge. After a further 20 m and shortly before the ruins of a wall, the path to Skógarkotsvegur branches off to the right. After crossing two streets, this riding trail leads you through a birch forest and past impressive faults which are covered with moss to the **Skógarkot** farm, which was abandoned in 1936. From a small hill there, you have a good panoramic view to **Thingvallavatn**.

Returning, go along the Gönguvegur in the direction of **Thingvallabaer**. After ½ hr, you will cross the street again and go in the direction of **Flossagjá** and then along the access road to the church. From the church, a path leads further along an access road to the hotel and back to the **starting point** of our tour.

The Allmannagjá gorge is the geological border between Europe and America.

48 Krisuvík thermal area

A spectacular circular tour through an undeveloped hot spring area

Parking lot – Graenavatn – Litla Lambafell – parking lot

Location: Reykjavik, 30 m.
Starting point: On Route 42 (coming from Reykjavik), there is a parking lot with kiosk on the right near a clearly noticeable steam spring. Approach: By car or possibly by bicycle on Route 42.
Walking time: 2½ – 3 hrs.
Ascent: 150 m.
Grade: Hike, partially without trails, through

a solfataric region.
Accommodation: In Reykjavik.
Alternative route: The starting point of this hike can also be reached from Reykjavik by bicycle. Information on current bike rental at the visitor's office. Organized cycling tours are offered to the »Blue Lagoon« (warm lake for swimming).

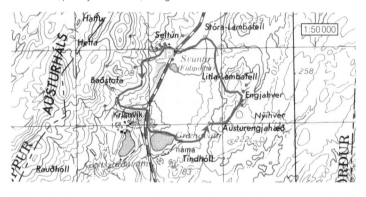

On the Reykjanes peninsula, which is unjustly avoided by many tourists, the Mid-Atlantic ridge reaches the surface. Fissures, volcanoes and geothermal areas with solfataras and mud pits show that this region is still volcanically active.

Next to the enclosed steam spring, a path which is made of wood leads you past several hot springs. From here, we climb up the left shoulder on a ground of scoria to a further solfataric field. Then go along the contour line until you are looking down on the hot spring area and the **Krisuvík** farm. The sheep trail runs along secure ground here. Keep to the left and cross a small shoulder and then keep to the ridge, which is covered with grass. Next to an artificial steam spring, you can see a lane. Here you should descend to the main road and then turn right. Near an old farm building, walk along Route 42 to the **Graenavatn**. On the bank we found a stone which made crossing the barbed wire easier. Afterwards, follow the path which runs parallel to a fence (which leads away from the shore) and go up a shoulder. From a distance, you can already see a rising column of steam. We go in this direction. Boiling lakes of mud, solfataras and hot springs create a fascinating thermal area. The descent begins to the left past **Litla Lambafell**. At a fork, we keep to the left until we come to the swampy meadow. At the edge of this, we go to the north until we reach a fence. We follow it back to the road. Across the road, we see the steaming geyser and thus the **starting point** of the hike.

The tour leads through a many-sided thermal area without paths.

49 Westmannaeyjar – Heimaey

A hike tracing the volcanic eruption

Border of town – Eldfell – starting point

Location: Heimaey, 10 m.
Starting point: Eastern border of the town of Heimaey. Approach: Ferry connection from Thorlákshöfn daily at 12:00 and Thursday, Friday and Sunday at 19:00, from Westmann's Island daily 8:15 and Thursday, Friday and Sunday at 15:30 or three air connections daily.
Walking time: 1 hr.

Ascent: 160 m.
Grade: The dormant volcano is easy to climb.
Accommodation: Camping, youth hostel, hotel in Heimaey.
Advice: The rocks which jut up steeply near the harbor are a good place to observe puffins.

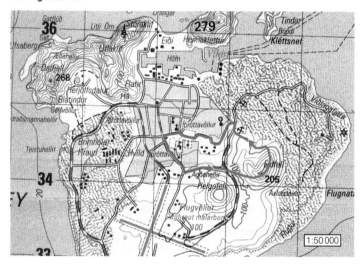

The island of Heimaey, which is only 6 km long and 3 km wide, was the scene of a dramatic rescue action in 1973 when the **Eldfell** Volcano suddenly erupted. Since Heimaey has a very important fishing harbor, the successful attempt was made at stopping the flow of lava using large amounts of cold ocean water. However, most houses were buried under a meter thick layer of ashes. If you go to Heimaey today, you will amazingly discover that there is little to be seen of the destructive effects of the volcanic eruption. Only the ruin of one house has been left standing and the rest of the town has been completely rebuilt.

Directly at the eastern **border of town**, a path leads up the **Eldfell**, which still steams slightly. After ½ hr, you will be standing on the highest point from which you have a good view of the entire island. From here, you can see the new field of lava in the northeast which tripled the size of the island and threatened the harbor.

On the other side, you descend and return to the **town**.

Houses near the new field of lava in Heimaey.

Skiing tours

Winter trips to Iceland are becoming more and more popular but you should keep in mind that skiing tours in the classical Alpine style are hardly possible in Iceland because there are no managed cabins and the small emergency cabins cannot be heated. In addition, you should take into account the extremely short days in winter and the difficulties with orientation in a large and treeless land. Those interested in winter tours should therefore inquire at the winter sports centers or the hiking clubs, which offer skiing tours from January to May. You can find current addresses at the Icelandic tourist offices.

The island appears to be less suitable for winter sports because of its temperate cold but wet winter climate. Nevertheless, there are some ski resorts (international code +354): Bláfjöll near Reykjavik: 561-8400 or 7700, Ísafjörthur: 456-3793 or 3125, Siglufjörthur: 467-1806, Ólafsfjörthur: 466-2527 or 2428, Dalvik: 466-1010 or 1005, Akureyri: 462-1806, Húsavik: 464-1873 or 1430, Oddskarth: 476-1465.

Especially in the time from May to June, there are nice possibilities for skiing tours in Iceland. For experienced short-carving skiers who are travelling with their own cars in June, it makes sense to take along your own equipment. However, short-carving skis with a steel edge and a sturdy binding or »Bigfoot« are imperative. (Alternative: We used an old Alpine ski with a »Bigfoot« binding which was shortened to 85 cm. These were not only light but also gave us sufficient support when combined with heavy hiking boots. However, you should definitely test it first!)

In the following section you will find a list of some of the most interesting possibilities for skiing tours.

■ **In the Akureyri region:** One of the most worthwhile tourist destinations of all is the Súlur, not only because this mountain offers an excellent view, but also because it provides an ideal slope. In the spring, you can climb the Súlur with hides, but in the early summer, hiking is better (compare Tour 34). Into July, there are good possibilities with short-carving skis. The Glerárdalur at the foot of the Súlur provides for good possibilities for skiing tours in the spring and there is an emergency cabin (Lambi) at the end of the valley. Above Akureyri, there is a small skiing area which lies across from the Súlur and can be reached by an access road. When there is little snow, we don't recommend climbing here because of swampy areas and the steepness of the landscape.

■ **In Landmannalaugar:** From **Bláhnúkur**, a snow-covered channel pulls down to the north and also has sufficient snow in summer. Skiing here is a worthwhile variation but we can only advise experienced and safe short-carving skiers to do so here because it is mostly very icy and is very steep.

- Summer skiing areas: In the highlands, you can find the popular **Kerlingarfjöll** skiing area which is also famous for its colorful liparite mountains. The summer ski resort with accommodations and rental of equipment is open from the end of June to the end of August. A four-wheel drive vehicle is required to reach it.
- Skiing tours on glaciers are offered on an individual basis (**Snaefells**, **Langjökull**). Usually, a tracked vehicle will take you up. The danger of crevasses in the glacier is difficult to estimate for non-natives. Therefore, you should never undertake a skiing tour of a glacier alone.

Short-carving from the Bláhnúkur.

Index

The numbers refer to the numbers of the walks